RELIGIONS
OF
MESOAMERICA

Volumes in the Religious Traditions of the World Series

Edited by H. Byron Earhart

Religions of Japan *by H. Byron Earhart*
Religions of China *by Daniel L. Overmyer*
Buddhism *by Robert C. Lester*
Hinduism *by David M. Knipe*
Judaism *by Michael A. Fishbane*
Christianity *by Sandra S. Frankiel*
Islam *by Frederick M. Denny*
Religions of Africa *by E. Thomas Lawson*
Native Religions of North America *by Åke Hultkrantz*
Religions of Mesoamerica *by David Carrasco*

Religions
of
Mesoamerica

Cosmovision and
Ceremonial Centers

DAVÍD CARRASCO

 HarperSanFrancisco
A Division of HarperCollins*Publishers*

Grateful acknowledgment is made for permission to reprint excerpts
from the following works: *The Broken Spears*, by Miguel Leon-Portilla, copyright © 1962 by Beacon Press; reprinted by permission of
Beacon Press. *Native Mesoamerican Spirituality*, edited by Miguel
Leon-Portilla, copyright © 1980 by Paulist Press; used by permission of Paulist Press. *People of the Bat*, edited by Carol Karasik,
copyright © 1988 by the Smithsonian Institution, Washington,
D.C.; reproduced by permission of the Smithsonian Institution
Press. *Popul Voh*, copyright © 1985 by Dennis Tedlock; reprinted
by permission of Simon & Schuster, Inc. *Florentine Codex; General
History of the Things of New Spain* by Bernardo de Sahagun, translated by Arthur S. Anderson and Charles E. Dibble, copyright © 1981
by University of Utah Press; used with permission.

Library of Congress Cataloging-in-Publication Data
Carrasco, Davíd.
   Religions of Mesoamerica: cosmovision and ceremonial centers
/David Carrasco. — 1st ed.
     p. cm.
   Includes bibliographical references.
   ISBN 0-06-061325-4
   1. Aztecs—Religion and mythology. 2. Mayas—Religion
and mythology. 3. Aztecs—Antiquities.
   4. Mayas—Antiquities. 5. Mexico—Antiquities.   I. Title.
F1219.76.R45C372   1990
299'.792—dc20   89-45990
                                          CIP

91 92 93 94 CWI 10 9 8 7 6 5 4 3 2

This book is dedicated to my parents
David and Marji Carrasco
El Cocotero y la Lechucita

Contents

Editor's Foreword   ix

Author's Note   xi

Acknowledgments   xiii

Preface   xv

Chronology   xxi

Chapter I. Introduction: Approaching Mesoamerican Religions   1

Inventions and Fantasies of Mesoamerica   1

Sources for Understanding: The Ensemble Approach to Evidence   11

Religion as Worldmaking, Worldcentering, Worldrenewing   19

Chapter II. History and Cosmovision in Mesoamerican Religions   24

Plants and the Sacred Dead   27

The Olmec World: Jaguars and Giants in Stone   30

Astronomy and the Sacred Ball Game   35

The Classic Maya: Kings and Cosmic Trees   37

Teotihuacan: The Imperial Capital   40

Tollan: City of the Plumed Serpent   43

Aztec War, Cosmic Conflict   45

The Mesoamerican Cosmovision   51

Chapter III. The Religion of the Aztecs: Ways of the Warrior, Words of the Sage   58

    The Sacred Career of Topiltzin Quetzalcoatl   59

    Cosmovision and the Human Body   65

    Serpent Mountain: The Great Aztec Temple   70

    Sacred Words   77

    Rites of Renewal and Human Sacrifice   85

Chapter IV. Maya Religion: Cosmic Trees, Sacred Kings, and the Underworld   92

    The Lost Civilization of the Maya   95

    The Cosmic Tree   98

    Sacred Kingship   103

    The Calendar and the Regeneration of Time   113

    The Ordeals of Xibalba   117

Chapter V. Mesoamerica as a New World: Colonialism and Religious Creativity   124

    The Social and Symbolic Crisis of the Colonial New World   127

    The Virgin of Guadalupe   135

    The Peyote Hunt of the Huichol Indians   138

    Dia de los Muertos (Day of the Dead)   142

    The Fiesta of Santiago Among the Tzutujil Maya   147

    Conclusions   153

Notes   159

Glossary   165

Selected Reading List   172

■

Religious Traditions of the World

One of human history's most fascinating aspects is the richness and variety of its religious traditions—from the earliest times to the present, in every area of the world. The ideal way to learn about all these religions would be to visit the homeland of each—to discuss the scriptures or myths with members of these traditions, explore their shrines and sacred places, view their customs and rituals. Few people have the luxury of leisure and money to take such trips, of course; nor are many prepared to make a systematic study of even those religions that are close at hand. Thus this series of books is a substitute for an around-the-world trip to many different religious traditions: it is an armchair pilgrimage through a number of traditions both distant and different from one another, as well as some situated close to one another in time, space, and religious commitment.

Individual volumes in this series focus on one or more religions, emphasizing the distinctiveness of each tradition while considering it within a comparative context. What links the volumes as a series is a shared concern for religious traditions and a common format for discussing them. Generally, each volume will explore the history of a tradition, interpret it as a unified set of religious beliefs and practices, and give examples of religious careers and typical practices. Individual volumes are self-contained treatments and can be taken up in any sequence. They are introductory, providing interested readers with an overall interpretation of religious traditions without presupposing prior knowledge.

The author of each book combines special knowledge of a religious tradition with considerable experience in teaching and communicating an interpretation of that tradition. This special knowledge includes familiarity with various languages, investigation of religious texts and historical development, and direct contact with the peoples and practices under study. The authors have refined their special knowledge through many years of teaching and writing to frame a general interpretation of the tradition that is responsible to the best-known facts and is readily available to the interested reader.

Let me join with the authors of the series in wishing you an enjoyable and profitable experience in learning about religious traditions of the world.

H. Byron Earhart
Series Editor

Author's Note

Throughout this book I use the spelling *Moctezuma* to refer to the Aztec rulers usually called, in English, *Montezuma*. There were two Moctezumas, Moctezuma Ilhuicamina 1440–1464 and Moctezuma Xocoyotzin 1502–1520. The Nahuatl spelling in the Florentine Codex is *Motecuzoma,* though some scholars use *Moteuczomah* while others use *Moteuczoma.* I am following the translation of Dibble and Anderson, who consistently use *Moctezuma.*

Acknowledgments

I want to thank the colleagues and friends who helped me during the writing of this book. They include Lois Middleton and Linda Cohen, who organized many important details of research; Peter van der Loo, Robert Carlsen, Carolyn Tate, and Anthony Aveni for advice on certain chapters; Scott Sessions for help with the codices; and Richard Griswold del Castillo and Jose (Dr. Loco) Cuellar for helping me direct the narrative for use in Chicano studies programs. William B. Taylor urged me to take a long second look at the presentation of colonialism and syncretism. Michio Araki, from the University of Tsukuba, Tsukuba, Japan, opened the resources of the Institute of Philosophy to me during the early drafts of this book. I thank him and the students who assisted me in library research while in the land of the rising sun. I also remember Jane Marie Swanberg.

This work has also been enriched by a number of scholars, who participate in summer seminars at the Mesoamerican Archive. They include Elizabeth Boone, Robert Bye, Charles Long, Jane Day, Johanna Broda, Edward Calnek, Doris Heyden, Cecelia Klein, Eduardo Matos Moctezuma, Alfredo Lopez Austin, Edelmira Linares, H. B. Nicholson, Richard Townsend, Jorge Klor de Alva, Lawrence Desmond, and Lawrence Sullivan. Paul Wheatley's work has nurtured this project from the beginning. Finally, my gratitute extends to Raphael and Fletcher Lee Moses for their timely and generous support.

David Carrasco
Boulder, Colorado
and
Tsukuba, Japan

Preface

Raise your spirit . . . Hear about the new discovery!
Peter Martyr, September 13, 1493

One of the momentous transformations in the history of the Western world took place on the shores and in the villages and cities of Mesoamerica between 1492 and 1521. This transformation was initiated with the voyages of Cristóbal Colón (we know him as Christopher Columbus) and reached a culmination, of sorts, with the fall of the Aztec capital, **Tenochtitlan,*** in 1521. Within three quick decades the European image of the world was radically changed and a previously unimaginable universe—Nueva España, America, and above all, the New World—was discovered, invaded, and invented. As Tzvetan Todorov notes, the discovery and conquest of Mesoamerica was the "most astonishing encounter of our history," which "heralds our present identity" as citizens of the world and interpreters of culture.[1]

We have the vantage point of a grand eyewitness account of a pivotal episode in this transformation provided by Bernal Díaz del Castillo, a sergeant in Cortés's invading army, who describes the Spanish *entrada* into the Aztec capital in 1519 this way:

> During the morning we arrived at a broad causeway and continued our march towards Iztapalapa and when we saw so many cities and villages built in the water and other great towns on dry land and that straight and level causeway going towards Mexico, we were amazed and said that it was like the enchantments they tell of in the legend of Amadis, on account of the great towers and buildings rising from the water, and all built of masonry. And some of the soldiers even asked whether the things that we saw were not a dream.

---

* Terms defined in the Glossary are printed in boldface where they first appear in text.

Once the Spaniards entered the city the palaces appeared even more amazing to their eyes.

> How spacious and well built they were, of beautiful stone work and cedar wood, and the wood of other sweet scented trees, with great rooms and courts, wonderful to behold, covered with awnings of cotton cloth.

And the natural world of the city was also wonderful.

> When we had looked well at all of this, we went to the orchard and garden, which was such a wonderful thing to see and walk in, that I was never tired of looking at the diversity of the trees, and noting the scent which each one had, and the paths full of roses and flowers, and the many fruit trees and native roses, and the pond of fresh water. There was another thing to observe, the great canoes were able to pass into the garden from the lake through an opening that had been made so that there was no need for their occupants to land. And all was cemented and very splendid with many kinds of stone (monuments) with pictures on them . . . I say again that I stood looking at it and thought that never in the world would there be discovered other lands such as these, for at that time there was no Peru, nor any thought of it. Of all these wonders that I then beheld today all is overthrown and lost, nothing left standing.[2]

This and other eyewitness accounts show that the Spaniards were astonished by the architectural wonders, agricultural abundance, royal luxuries, ritual violence, social stratification, and spatial organization of the capital. To their great surprise Mesoamerica was an urban civilization organized by powerful, pervasive religious beliefs and practices.

Within eighteen months, however, distrust, intrigue, torture, murder, and conquest dominated the interaction between Spaniard and Aztec. The last Aztec ruler, **Cuauhtemoc** (Diving Eagle), surrendered to Cortés and his army of Spaniards and Indian allies on November 15, 1521, at the ceremonial center of **Tlatelolco** in the capital. The Aztec view of the events leading up to this terrible change appear in this native lament:

> Broken spears lie in the road;
> we have torn our hair in our grief.
> The houses are roofless now, and their walls
> are red with blood.

We have pounded our hands in despair
against the adobe walls,
for our inheritance, our city, is lost and dead.
The shields of our warriors were its defense,
but they could not save it. . . .

They set a price on all of us
on the young men, the priests, the boys and the girls
the price of a poor man was only two handfuls of corn
or ten cakes made from mosses or twenty cakes
of salty couch-grass.
Gold, jade, rich cloths, quetzal feathers—
everything that once was precious was now considered
worthless.[3]

In spite of the human devastation and cultural transformation
brought on by the conquest and European colonialism, significant
versions of the native images of space, time, the cosmos, social and
economic relations, and the underworld are available to us. The ar-

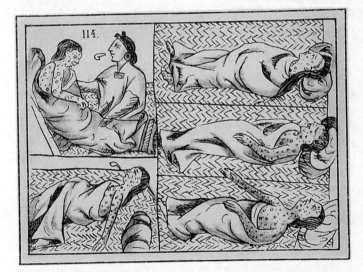

These panels come from the Florentine Codex *and they depict the suffering and
medical care of smallpox victims. The Spanish brought to Mexico with them a
number of foreign diseases that devastated the indigenous population in a very
short time. Sahagun (Paso y Troncoso ed.)*

chaeological, ethnohistorical, and literary evidence provides us with the eloquent statement that the story of Mesoamerican religions is the story of cities and symbols of cities. In fact Mesoamerica was a world organized by hundreds of carefully planned **ceremonial centers** and scores of monumental, even majestic cities and city-states. It is usually overlooked that Mesoamerica was one of the seven places on the globe—with China, Mesopotamia, Egypt, Indus Valley, Nigeria, and Peru—where human culture managed the great transformation from pre-urban society to urban society. These urban societies, while different from one another in many ways, all developed traditions of art, symbolism, politics, and social organization that became the heart and nexus of human culture. It is also remarkable that in each of these seven cases of **primary urban generation** the societies at large were *regulated and organized by monumental ceremonial centers that contained such architectural structures as temples, platform mounds, pyramids, palaces, terraces, staircases, courts, stelae, and spacious ritual precincts.*[4] The little footprints crossing the ancient Mesoamerican maps and the portrayal of ritual life in the art of various cities show that ancient peoples visited such places as **Teotihuacan**, Abode of the Gods; Xochicalco, Place of the House of Flowers; Chichén Itzá, Mouth of the Well of the Itza; Colhuacan, Place of the Ancestors; **Tollan**, Place of Reeds; and Teocolhuacan, Place of the Divine Ancestors. In this way ancient Mesoamerican history is the story of people and their symbols moving to and from cities and their ceremonial centers.

This urban image of place and action provides the plan for this book. The controlling idea for the entire study is that the ceremonial precincts of Mesoamerica were the centers and theaters for the acting out of religious and social life. These ceremonial centers served as powerful magnets attracting people, goods, authority, and sacred forces into their precincts, ceremonies, and marketplaces. Once within the power, drama, and order of the ceremonial center people and their goods underwent experiences that changed them and their sense of orientation and value. But these ceremonial centers, operating under the control of royal and priestly elites, also had a *centrifugal* force, which redistributed goods, values, and people outward into the society at large.

The second important term in the subtitle is **cosmovision,** which means the ways in which Mesoamericans *combined their cosmological notions relating to time and space into a structured and systematic worldview.* This worldview included a strong sense of parallelism between the celestial, supernatural forces of the cosmos (macrocosmos) and the biological, human patterns of life on earth (microcosmos). As we shall see, the spatial organization, architecture, and calendrical rituals of many ceremonial centers in Mesoamerican history expressed intimate parallels between the time and space of the deities and the time and space of humans and terrestrial beings. One of the most important points to understand at the outset is that in Mesoamerican religions *time* and *space* were inseparable realities.

Chapter 1 surveys the challenge of studying Mesoamerican religions and the rich ensemble of resources available for the study of Mesoamerican religions. It discusses three characteristics of religious history in Mesoamerica: worldmaking (cosmovision and sacred space), worldcentering (cosmovision and the human body), and worldrenewing (the ceremonial rejuvenation of time, human life, agriculture, and the gods). Chapter 2 develops a historic overview of the diversity and richness of major ceremonial centers and ritual traditions in Mesoamerican culture. It begins with the artistic and trading achievements of the Olmecs (1500–200 BCE); outlines the superb creativity of Classic Maya ceremonial life (200–900 CE); discusses the grand imperial capital of Teotihuacan (200–750 CE); outlines the utopian image of **Quetzalcoatl**'s kingdom in Tollan (900–1200 CE); and ends with the religious world of the Aztec empire (1325–1521 CE). Chapter 3 focuses on the religion of the warrior: the power of ritual violence in Aztec religion expressed in the cult of the warrior, warrior kings, and the sacrificial ceremonies at the Great Aztec Temple of Tenochtitlan. This chapter alos includes a discussion of the art of Aztec speech. Chapter 4 explores the "blood of kings," that is, the royal religion of Maya ceremonial settlements that were organized around the symbolism of the flowering sacred tree and the careers of royal families and their ancestors.[5] In this discussion of the Maya achievement we will examine one of the most pervasive meanings of all Mesoamerican religions: the sacred powers of agricultural life. Chapter 5 summarizes several continuities and innovations in Mesoamerican religions during the colonial period and in contemporary communities. We will discuss the New World as a world of social and spiritual crisis for indigenous and *mestizo* (mixed Spanish/Indian parentage) peoples. We will look at an array of religious expressions of worldmaking (Huichol peyote hunt), worldcentering (Day of the Dead ceremonies), and worldrenewing (cults of Guadalupe and Santiago). In this array we will see clear examples of both religious pilgrimages and religious **syncretism**.

Chronology of Mesoamerican Religions

Dates	Major Events
30,000–6500 BCE	Groups of peoples from northeast Asia enter the Americas through Bering Strait land bridge bringing hunting cultures, shamanism, and animal ceremonialism.
6500–1500 BCE	Incipient agricultural development focusing on maize, beans and squashes, cotton, and chili peppers leads to village formation and the importance of religious cults associated with rain and fertility. Settlement in villages with ceremonial centers, burial mounds, and sacred rulers.
1500–900 BCE	Rise of Olmec civilization centered on eastern coast of Mesoamerica in humid lowlands of Veracruz and Tabasco and spreading into western and southern Mesoamerica. The appearance of monumental architecture

characterized by a superb sculptural tradition in gigantic basalt monuments and miniature jade work. Examples include the "Colossal Heads" of San Lorenzo and the hybrid art style of animal (jaguar, bird, reptile) and human forms demonstrating the importance of shamanic specialists. The rise of intense social stratification.

900–300 BCE

Florescence of Olmec cosmovision and ceremonial style throughout parts of Mesoamerica. Formation of the monumental ceremonial center of La Venta, where rich burials reveal intense social stratification. Proliferation of religious cults dedicated to gods of rain, fire, maize, Plumed Serpent, the Earth, and the Underworld.

600–300 BCE

Formation of monumental ceremonial center at Monte Albán in Oaxaca, with evidence of astronomical alignments of ceremonial buildings, elaborate public ceremonies, and royal tombs.

Rise of Iztapan civilization in Chiapas, where eighty pyramidal mounds, upright stelae, Long Count calendar dates, and writing appear,

	indicating that the Mesoamerican cosmovision is generalized.
300 BCE–100 CE	Early formation of the Maya civilization in Petén area of south-central Mesoamerica. Sites at Uaxactun, Yaxchilán, El Mirador, and Tikal take shape.
200–900 CE	The Classic Period. Mesoamerican culture is integrated in a number of major areas: Teotihuacan in the central plateau, Maya cultures of the lowlands, and Monte Albán in Oaxaca.
100–700 CE	Teotihuacan becomes the imperial capital of an empire. This four-quartered city with towering pyramids, palaces, stairways, marketplaces, and monumental sculpture demonstrates that the cosmovision has become imprinted on the entire urban form. Cults of rain, war, jaguars, Feathered Serpent, stars develop. Also, the great ceremonial city of Cholula, organized by the largest pyramid on earth, develops during this period. Other important sites include Xochicalco and El Tajin.

300–900 CE	The extravagant cosmovision of the classic Maya develops in the lowlands. This cosmovision includes the Long Count calendar; intense presentation of royal families; complex writing system; and rich but scattered ceremonial centers at Tikal, Yaxchilán, Palenque, Uxmal, Copán, Quiriguá, and elsewhere are flourishing. The cosmovision of the cosmic tree, dynastic records, the journey through Xibalba, autosacrifice, and human sacrifice appear in iconography.
830–900 CE	Collapse of segments of Maya civilization
900–1500 CE	Post-Classic Mesoamerica. The rise and fall of the Toltec Empire and the development of the Aztec world. Also ceremonial centers at Mitla in Oaxaca and Chichén Itzá are flourishing.
900–1100 CE	The Toltec Empire centered at Tollan (Tula), famous for the Quetzalcoatl tradition. Iconography reveals presence of warrior cults, long-distance trading, and the prestige of having originated and perfected the arts, astronomy, and a cosmovision that influenced subsequent cultures. Chichén

	Itzá in Yucatan flourishes and integrates Toltec traditions.
1200–1350 CE	Migrating farmers and warriors move into the Lake Cultures of the central plateau, which have been developing during Teotihuacan and the Toltec Empire. Chichimecas (the Aztecs) partially assimilate with existing social patterns of farming, warfare, market exchange, and religious cults.
1325 CE	Chichimecas (the Aztecs) settle the swampy island of Tenochtitlan led by their deity, Huitzilopochtli, in the form of an eagle. The settlement is eventually divided into four great quarters surrounding the temple Coatepec (Serpent Mountain), and over seventy-five ceremonial buildings. The cults of Tlaloc, god of agriculture and water, and Huitzilopochtli, god of war and tribute, are combined at the Great Temple.
1350 CE	Another Chichimec group settles the nearby island of Tlatelolco, which becomes the market center for the Lake Cultures. Also the site of a great ceremonial center.
1425–1428 CE	The Mexicas, under the leadership of warriors, lead the

	rebellion against the city-state of Azcapotzalco and form the Triple Alliance of Tenochtitlan. Tlacopan, and Texcoco, which rules central Mesoamerica.
1440–1468 CE	The Aztec Tlatoani Moctezuma Ilhuicamina rules and expands Coatepec, the great temple, the monumental ceremonial center in the capital, the tribute network, and warfare efforts. Eventually the city is populated by over 200,000 people.
1473 CE	The Aztecs of Tenochtitlan impose their rule on Tlatelolco and take control of the great market system, solidifying the core of their empire.
1503 CE	Moctezuma Xocoyotzin comes to the throne.
1510 CE	Spaniards begin reconnaissance along East Coast in Mexico.
1521 CE	Tenochtitlan falls when Cuahutemoc surrenders to Cortés at Tlatelolco.
1531 CE	Juan Diego experiences the apparition of the virgin of Guadalupe at Tepeyac.
1737 CE	Virgin of Guadalupe made patronness of Mexico.

1754 CE   Pope Benedict XIV officially
                                 recognizes Our Lady of
                                 Guadalupe.

1790 CE   Aztec calendar stone, also
                                 known as sun stone, discovered
                                 beneath the street in Mexico
                                 City.

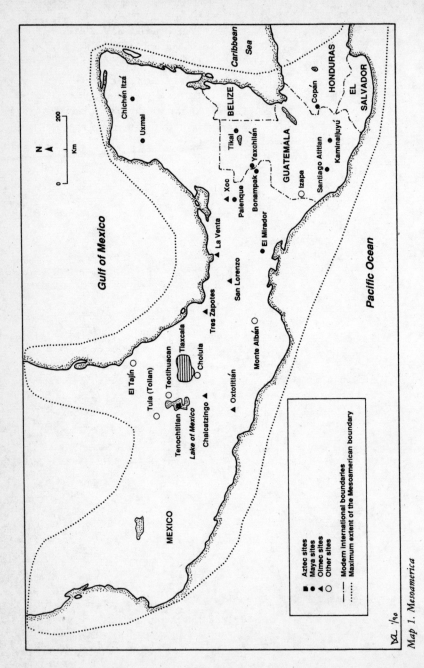

Map 1. Mesoamerica

CHAPTER I

Introduction: Approaching Mesoamerican Religions

Inventions and Fantasies of Mesoamerica

Around 1510 a Spanish reconnaissance expedition from the island of Cuba made contact with a small group of Maya Indians on a beach bordering territory that the people called the Land of the Turkey and the Deer. Attempting to figure out their location the Spaniards shouted, "What is this place called?" The natives replied, *"Uic athan,"* meaning, "We do not understand your words." In an ironic turn of meaning characteristic of many changes that were to follow, the Spaniards decided to call this area Yucatan, a place name that is now the permanent designation for this eastern part of Mesoamerica.[1]

Mesoamerica is a term given by scholars to designate a geographical and cultural area covering the southern two-thirds of mainland Mexico, Guatemala, Belize, El Salvador, and parts of Honduras, Nicaragua, and Costa Rica. In this area the powerful processes of urban generation began with sophisticated agricultural production in the second millennium BCE and ended with the Spanish conquest in the sixteenth century CE. Extensive research shows that Mesoamerica was inhabited by a wide spectrum of social groups with various levels of social integration; but the permanent, extensive ceremonial centers at the heart of social worlds resembling small-scale city-states became the most powerful social unit in a few different regions beginning around 1500 BCE. It is also clear that the earliest and most influential institutions contributing to the organization of peoples into urban centers were sacred ceremonial precincts. Therefore it is useful to approach the study of

Mesoamerican religions through the continuous patterns and presence for cosmovision and ritual action created and celebrated within these ceremonial centers and their city-states.

As the naming of Yucatan suggests, however, knowledge of these places and peoples was subject to inventions and fantasies that have had long-term influences. Unless we acknowledge their presence, they can silently distort our understanding of religion in Mesoamerican cultures. In fact Mesoamerica was a powerful European fantasy long before it was mapped or lived in. It was believed to be at once the Garden of Eden and the land of wild men, monstrosities, and devil worship. As the quote that opens the preface to this book indicates, there was excitement and even euphoria in Europe at the news of Columbus's landfall. This excitement extended beyond the Italian humanist Peter Martyr, as indicated by the fact that Columbus's first letter to the crown was published nine times in 1493 and twenty times by 1500. However, it was not easy or comfortable for Europeans to fit the incredible news of entirely unknown lands, peoples, empires, souls, gold, into their intellectual horizon. America became, for centuries, a "strange new world" with different languages, customs, symbols, cuisines, philosophies, manners, and landscapes. Juxtaposed to Peter Martyr's happy announcement is the cleric Cornelius De Pauw's claim, three hundred years later, that the "discovery of the New World was the most calamitous event in human history."[2]

Europeans struggled in diverse ways to observe, perceive, and understand the New World of America. In the process they produced many inventions and fantasies. The many inventions and fantasies concerning Mesoamerica can be divided into two groups: fantasies about Mesoamerican geography and inventions about the nature of human beings. It is important to review these fantasies and inventions before we study the religions of the Aztecs, Mayas, their neighbors, and contemporary religious expressions. This will help us see how Mesoamerican peoples and places were both attractive and threatening to European consciousness. It is important to be aware of this powerful ambivalence concerning religions and peoples in the New World so we can lessen its influence in our approach to Mesoamerican cultures, religious practices, and creativity. It is also important to recognize the religious themes that were woven into the European inventions about Mesoamerica.

This stylized map of the Aztec world depicts Tenochtitlan where an eagle is perched on a prickly pear cactus in the center of the four quadrants. Warriors with shields and flint-studded clubs are shown next to two conquered communities, represented by smoking temples and tilted and thatched roofs. From the Codex Mendoza, *a post-conquest manuscript prepared by the first viceroy of New Spain.*

Mesoamerica as an Earthly Paradise

From their first sightings of the "Indies" to the end of the sixteenth century, Europeans hoped they had discovered an earthly paradise filled with the Garden of Eden, the Seven Enchanted Cities of Gold, and the Fountain of Youth. These wonderful images had been deposited in European traditions for centuries, and it made sense to compare the exotic reports of the explorers with these fabulous places. It is significant that two major English literary works, Shakespeare's *The Tempest* and Thomas More's *Utopia,* reflect the fantasy that Europe was going to be renewed and transformed for the good by the settlement of the New World. We see the energy of this fantasy in Miranda's lines to Prospero in the last scene of *The Tempest.* In describing her "vision of the island" (at once Naples and America) she states,

> MIRANDA: O Wonder!
> How many goodly creatures are there here!
> How beauteous mankind is.
> O, brave new world, that has such people in't.
> PROSPERO: Tis new to thee. (Act 5, Scene 1)

While classical and European society had long dreamed and written about ideal social societies where human possibility could be fulfilled, Thomas More's image of Utopia (meaning "good place" and "no place") reflects the renewed sense that the dream was about to be realized in America. In fact the narrator of *Utopia,* Ralph Hythloday, was portrayed as the companion of Amerigo Vespucci, the Italian explorer who was credited with concluding in 1507 that the landmass of South America was not part of Asia, but was in fact a new continent. For this insight America was named after him.

The voyages of discovery stimulated both great interest and defensiveness on the part of Europeans, whose maps of geography and of humankind were being quickly and radically challenged. On the one hand there seemed to be "newness" coming in many forms. New lands, peoples, languages, colors, animals, vegetation, and religions were appearing on the European frontier. On the other hand these novelties appeared so "other," different, and—in Europeans' views—undeveloped that the Europeans felt the peoples of the New World of America had not evolved or progressed as they believed their own culture had.

All this evoked some important questions: What is a human being? What is the difference between a civilized and a barbaric language? Is Europe the center of the world? We can see this new ambivalence in a passage from the 1512 edition of Pomponius Mela's *Cosmographia*. The humanist Cochlaeus wrote in the Introduction,

> In our lifetime, Amerigo Vespucci is said to have discovered that New World with ships belonging to the kings of Spain and Portugal; he sailed not only beyond the torrid zone but far beyond the Tropic of Capricorn. He says Africa stretches as far: and that his New World is quite distinct from it and bigger than our Europe. Whether this is true or a lie, it has nothing . . . to do with Cosmography and the knowledge of History. For the peoples and places of that continent are unknown and unnamed to us and sailings are only made there with the greatest dangers. Therefore it is of no interest to geographers at all.[3]

In other words the discovery of a new continent was not about to alter the European map of the world as presented in school textbooks!

The landscape of the islands near Mexico and the beauty of the South American mainland stimulated stories that the earthly paradise written of in the Bible and medieval books had finally been discovered. Reports passed through European capitals that the land was indeed inhabited by humans who had not changed since the time of Adam and Eve. A quarter of a century later, in central Mexico, these hopes took the form of a belief that a **millennial kingdom** ruled by priests who would convert the masses of natives into Christians was about to be established. Franciscan missionaries believed they faced the opportunity to create an earthly Christian community that would fulfill New Testament prophecies and herald the return of Jesus Christ on earth. The belief that the place of the Aztec capital was central to this biblical event was symbolized by the arrival, in a grand ceremony in the spring of 1524, of twelve Franciscan priests (referred to as the "apostles") into Mexico City. It was thought they were reenacting the presence of the twelve disciples on earth and heralding the dawn of a heavenly kingdom. In subsequent decades some members of this order organized their Indian followers (whom they considered "like angels" or "soft wax" waiting for the impression of Christ on their hearts) into utopian communities to prepare the way for the end of time and the Second Coming of Jesus. A related belief, sometimes preached from pulpits in Mexico, was that the Apostle Thomas, the wandering disciple of Christ, had preached in Mexico fifteen centuries before, introducing Christian teachings that had subsequently been distorted with time. Both the hope in a millennial kingdom and the belief that Saint Thomas had preached in the New World centuries before reflected the primary attitude of the Catholic church toward the native peoples. They were "souls to be saved" in a global process of conversion.

The Mesoamerican landscape was also considered an abundant resource of gold. The desire for wealth resulted in extraordinary fantasies and tragedies in the settling of New Spain. Stories of El Dorado (cities of silver and gold), and rumors of **Moctezuma's** buried treasure motivated otherwise rational human beings to face immense challenges and dangers in search of mineral resources for a luxurious and powerful life. Consider this eyewitness account made by Aztec survivors of the conquest.

> And when they were given these presents (of gold, quetzal feathers, and golden necklaces), the Spaniards burst into smiles; their eyes shone with pleasure; they were delighted by them. They picked up the gold and fingered it like monkeys; they seemed to be transported by joy, as if their hearts were illumined and made new.
>
> The truth is that they longed and lusted for gold. Their bodies swelled with greed, and their hunger was ravenous. They hungered like pigs for the gold . . . They were like one who speaks a barbarous tongue: everything they said was in a barbarous tongue.[4]

This belief in Moctezuma's treasure of gold resurfaced again in Mexico City in 1982, when rumors spread that the archaeologists excavating the Great Aztec Temple had found the gold and were keeping it secret.

The Noble Savage/Wild Man

The most influential and degrading fantasy was the belief in the natural inferiority of the Indians. Some Europeans believed that the indigenous peoples were halfway between beasts and humans. American Indians were portrayed, in the first decades after the discovery of the New World, as cannibals, sexually promiscuous, lawless, and misdirected by pagan gods. They were, in short, humans, but wild humans whose evolution and development had taken a very different direction than did the civilizations that led to European cultures.

Other Europeans, however, argued that while these beings were indeed savages, they had not yet suffered the debilitating effects of civilization associated with greed, cruelty, and bad manners. Rather than being a wild human race they felt that the Indians were noble and pure in their hearts but still savages. Research has taught us that both these images, the wild man and the noble savage, were already deeply embedded in the European mind before Mesoamerica was discovered.

A third response to the natives of Mesoamerica became apparent as the sixteenth century unfolded and more contact between the Old World and the New World took place. A number of Spaniards realized that a complex mystery, a radically different world, was being revealed, which demanded careful and sustained analysis. This group became determined to discover where the Indians fit into the scheme of creation, society, and religion. For all three groups of European interpreters, Mesoamerica became the big screen upon which Europeans could either project these fantasies and at the same time believe these projections were realities, or carry out their comparative experiments in thinking and classification.

Treatment of native peoples became so brutal and dehumanizing, justified in part by these racial stereotypes, that in 1550 Charles V of Spain suspended all expeditions to America and summoned into session a *junta* of foremost theologians. This Council of the Fourteen, in Valladolid, Spain, was called to consider a debate on the question of whether it is "lawful for the King to wage war on the Indians before preaching the faith to them in order to subject them to his rule, so that afterwards, they may more easily be instructed in the faith."[5] The debate focused on two major questions: (1) What is the true nature of the Indian? and (2) Could Europeans justifiably use coercion, violence, and war to eliminate Indian religions and force the people to become Christians and obey the Spaniards?

This "Great Debate," as Lewis Hanke calls it in *Aristotle and the American Indians*, set in motion the written expression of ideas and racial prejudices that some people still use today in naming and interpreting Native American life and culture. At the heart of this conflict was a religious bias that Aztec and Maya religions were "ancient idolatries and false religion with which the devil was worshiped until the Holy Gospel was brought to this land."[6]

On one side of the debate was the Spanish philosopher **Juan Ginés de Sepulveda,** admirer of Cortés, friend of Erasmus, and translator of Aristotle's *Poetics* into Latin. He argued in a five-hundred-page treatise that the Indians were "as inferior to Spaniards . . . as children to adults, as women to men. . . . as great a difference between them . . . as monkeys to men."[7] Therefore the natural condition of the Indians was social slavery and obedience to the more rational Europeans. In other words Indians, by *nature,* not as a result of military weakness, deserved an eternally inferior social position in the New World. Further, any Indian refusal to obedience and the acceptance of a life of servitude was seen as the reasonable basis for using force, violence, and warfare against them. Lodged within this argument of Aristotelian logic is a destructive, grandiose conception of European superiority, perfection, and virtue. Conquerors never had it so good!

The Indian side was taken by the Dominican priest **Bartolomé de las Casas** (no native Mesoamericans were present), who had served as the Bishop of Chiapas while ministering in Maya communities. His extensive defense of the Indians contains aggressive discussions of such categories as "barbarian," "city," "Christian," "language," and "natural slavery" as a means to argue that preconquest Indian societies met all the Aristotelian criteria for a civil society. He argued that the people he saw every day were rational beings and should be brought to Christianity through persuasion, not violence. "Every man can become a Christian," he argued, because they already displayed a "wild" Christianity. Therefore there was no basis for a just war against the natives. Las Casas advanced the idea—which astonished many Spaniards during his day—that the American Indians compared favorably with peoples in ancient Old World civilizations, were eminently rational beings, and in fact fulfilled every one of Aristotle's requirements for the good life. He even argued that the Greeks and Romans were inferior to the Indians in child rearing, education of children, marriage arrangements, law, and architecture, and that the Indians were in some ways superior to the Spaniards.

Two points must be made about the way this kind of debate influences our attempts to understand the aesthetic, ritual, and cosmovision of Mesoamerican religions. First, a terrible alienation has already been set in motion whenever a society debates whether others "are human and do we have the right to kill them?" Subsequent generations are faced with the task of either elaborating these positions, or eliminating them so genuine methods of understanding and caring for the "others" can be developed. These debates in Spain, and in New Spain during the sixteenth century, took place long before the settlements of the New England colonies. The categories, prejudices, and clichés about Mesoamerican peoples were often the basis for the attitudes and policies of discrimination later developed toward American Indians in North America. Second, even though we may all wish to side with las Casas, it must be noted that both he and Sepulveda argued that the Indians must be changed into Christians in order to take a fully human place in society. Las Casas argued that the most impressive feature of the Indians was their similarity to Christians! Neither the priest nor the philosopher displayed a fundamental ability to appreciate these peoples for their own cultural style and content. Yet it is important to repeat that there were a number of people like las Casas and especially José de Acosta, author of a remarkable work, *Historia Natural y Moral de las Indies,* who did believe in the essential sameness of all human minds and made admirable efforts to figure out how the Indian world worked and how it could be reasonably related to the European worldview and life-style.

Clearly all European involvements with Mesoamerican cultures were not negative. While there were widespread attempts to degrade Indian art, clothes, cuisine, length of hair, and so on, there were also expressions of curiosity and admiration among a number of theologians, artists, and priests. Subsequent centuries have shown a remarkable interest in Mesoamerican art, politics, social structure, and religious practices. As Benjamin Keen has shown in *The Aztec Image in Western Thought,* Mesoamerica has been much on the minds of playwrights, poets, novelists, and painters as well as scholars. Among the significant cultural figures who have been drawn to Mesoamerican cultures for political, cultural, and intellectual materials are the German naturalist, traveler, and statesman Alexander von Humboldt; philosopher and writer Johann Gottfried von Herder; anthropologist E. B. Tylor; poet and critic Heinrich Heine, poet William Carlos Williams, English poet John Dryden; Napoleon Bonaparte; writer Hart Crane, and others.

Two Controversies

Two major controversies have been advanced in recent years, allowing for more fruitful understanding of the Mayas, the Aztecs, and their precursors. The first was whether or not Mesoamerican peoples attained a level of social and symbolic complexity associated with urban civilizations. The second was why human sacrifice and cannibalism took place on such a large scale.

Each of these issues, one concerning the social organization of Mesoamerica, the other concerning the ritual traditions of the Aztecs and Mayas, has involved heated and sometimes fantastic formulations. For instance in his article, "Montezuma's Dinner," written in 1876, one of the founders of cultural anthropology, Lewis H. Morgan, claimed that the Aztecs were "still a breech cloth people wearing the rag of barbarism as the unmistakable evidence of their condition." The intellectual milieu of Morgan's generation was inspired by the evolutionary framework of Charles Darwin and his followers, some of whom attempted to extend the new picture of biological development to the development of societies. Morgan had developed a scheme of human society's progress through three stages—savage, barbarism, and civilized—and argued that the Aztecs and their neighbors had only developed to the stage of barbarism. He argued that the Aztec palaces described by Hernan Cortés and Bernal Díaz del Castillo were, according to Morgan (who could see it all more clearly 350 years later), "joint tenement houses" that "reflected the weakness of the Indian family and ability to face alone the struggle of life." That the barbarian chief Moctezuma might have eaten on a tablecloth scandalized Morgan, who wrote, "There was neither a political society nor a state, nor any civilization in America, when it was discovered and excluding the Eskimo, but one race of Indians, the Red Race."[8]

Although Morgan's thesis was very influential well into the twentieth century, subsequent research by archaeologists and ethnohistorians have shown that it is not a question of whether Native Americans developed cities or not, but of what kinds of cities they did develop. In fact scholars have discovered a number of striking similarities between Mesoamerican cities and the urban civilizations of China, Egypt, Mesopotamia, India, Nigeria, and Peru.

More recently, in 1979, a furious controversy broke out in academic journals and books concerning what Marvin Harris called the "Cannibal Kingdom" of the Aztecs. Again, as in Morgan's day, the general intellectual atmosphere influenced the interpretation of the specifics of Mesoamerican culture in a distorted fashion. Anthropological literature in the 1970s was awash with the theory of cultural materialism, an approach that tended to reduce cultural developments to the material conditions and forces in society. At the center of this debate were the extraordinary ritual practices of bloodletting, human sacrifice, and ritual cannibalism practiced by Mesoamerican peoples. The debate divided into two camps: (1) the ecological explanation, which stated that "they ate humans for protein and profit"; and (2) the cultural explanation, which stated that "they were ritually exchanging gifts in the forms of thighs, hearts, skulls, and blood." But neither of these approaches was solidly based on Aztec or Maya conceptions of matter, the human body, or human/diety relations. As we shall see Mesoamerican religions were animated, in part, by ritual bloodletting and the sacrifice of human beings, who were ritually transformed into deities. But neither of these explanations was based on a secure understanding of what these peoples actually did and what they meant when they did it. We will study these unusual practices in chapters 3 and 4.

Sources for Understanding: The Ensemble Approach to Evidence

In 1982 a Mexican journalist visiting France was given permission to study the Aztec ritual manuscript the *Tonalamatl Aubin* in the confines of the rare books room at the National Library in Paris. With a certain stealth and unusual luck he stole the manuscript from the museum and fled to Yucatan, Mexico, where he was eventually tracked down by Interpol. He announced in the newspapers that the precious manuscript had been illegally taken from Mexico in 1840 and that he had returned an indigenous treasure to its homeland. While the two governments disputed the rightful ownership of the *Aubin* the journalist became something of a national hero. Today the manuscript is in Biblioteca Nacional in Mexico City.

The cultural pride associated with the recovery of the *Tonalamatl Aubin* symbolizes some of the problems and possibilities facing the study of Mesoamerican religions. On the one hand we are faced with the scattered remnants of the pictorial, archaeological, and literary evidence. Hernan Cortés's march from Villa Rica de la Vera Cruz to Tenochtitlan was punctuated with the defacing, whitewashing, and removal of religious monuments and images. In case after case the Spaniards destroyed the images of deities and ceremonial life, replacing them with Christian crosses on the spot. Later, in 1535, the apostolic inquisitor of Mexico, Juan de Zumarraga, ordered the collection and destruction of the pictorial records belonging to the Nahuatl cultural capital of Texcoco. Tradition tells us that the beautiful painted historical, ritual, and genealogical screenfolds were gathered into a huge pile in the local marketplace, set afire, and turned to ashes. It is a bitter fact that of the hundreds of pictorial manuscripts extant in Mesoamerica in 1517 only eleven remain today.

On the other hand extensive archaeological discoveries, excellent reproductions of the existing pictorials, recent translations of Maya script and Nahuatl documents, and an abundance of ethnohistorical writings composed in the sixteenth and seventeenth centuries provide us with revealing accounts of religious patterns and practices from a variety of local city-states in different parts of Mesoamerica. In addition there are millions of Nahuatl- and Maya-speaking people alive today who know elements of the ancient cosmovision and practice religious rituals in ceremonial centers that have dimensions of pre-Hispanic symbolism.

Given this abundant evidence the most useful approach to the study of Mesoamerican religions is an ensemble approach: the integration of a variety of types of evidence including pictorial manuscripts like the *Codex Borgia* and *Codex Mendoza;* ritual objects like the masks and statues of the Great Aztec Temple; the Aztec Calendar Stone; myths like the *Leyenda de los Soles* or the *teocuitl* (divine song) of the birth of the Aztec war god Huitzilopochtli; carvings like the reliefs from the Maya cities of Yaxchilán and

Palenque; archaeological material such as the excavations at Copán, Tlatelolco, Teotihuacan, Cacaxtla, or Rio Azul; ethnohistorical descriptions such as those found in Diego de Landa's *Relacíon de las Cosas de Yucatan,* Diego Durán's *Book of the Gods and Rites and the Ancient Calendar,* or extensive mythologies found, for instance, in the Maya book **Popul Vuh.** Rather than approaching religion from the privileged position of the star performance of one text, say a pictorial manuscript or a Spanish eyewitness account, we will combine four kinds of evidence: archaeological records, literary testimony, pictorial manuscripts, and contemporary fieldwork reports.

Archaeological Records

Archaeological discoveries have uncovered major ritual artifacts and large portions of ceremonial centers from numerous Mesoamerican cultures during the last three hundred years. In 1790, for instance, the Great Aztec Calendar Stone was uncovered below a street in Mexico City revealing the Aztec cosmogony, or story of the ages of the universe. Later, in 1841, John L. Stephens and Frank Catherwood, after exploring and drawing a number of Maya ceremonial centers long abandoned and covered by the jungle, published *Incidents of Travel in Central America, Chiapas, and Yucatan, Mexico.* They startled the English-speaking world with their reports of pyramids, tombs, ball courts, and huge statues of lavishly dressed lords and gods. Stephens actually purchased the ruins of the ancient city of Copán for thirty-five dollars! In 1810 Alexander von Humboldt published valuable paintings and reports of his visits to numerous Mexican ruins and awakened in German universities and other parts of Europe a real interest in visiting and studying Mesoamerican society. Between 1900 and 1915 Mexican archaeologists uncovered the great pyramids of Teotihuacan, showing the truly monumental nature of an ancient capital. In the following decades Mexican archaeologists discovered tombs, temples, pyramids, ball courts, and palaces in such cities as Monte Albán, Xochicalco, Quirigua, Palenque, Tikal, Tula, Copán, Yaxchilán, and El Mirador. During the last twenty years a veritable revolution in our view of the ancient Maya has been accomplished, in part through archaeological and iconographic analysis of sculptured images and written inscriptions. Information about the daily life, political alliances, astronomical influences, crafts, dynastic privilege, and cosmovision of the **Classic Maya** is increasing every month. Another major development has been the excellent reproductions of the Mixtec pictorials by publishing houses in Europe. Each of these discoveries has yielded extensive information on the cities, architecture, and ritual actions in Mesoamerica.

Among the most significant archaeological discoveries in this century, reflecting the interplay between the religious imagination and urban centers, was the 1978 to 1983 excavation of the Great Aztec Temple of Tenochtitlan in Mexico City. This temple, called **Coatepec** or Mountain of the Serpent, was located in the center of the ancient capital. But it was not only the political and symbolic center of the Aztec empire, it was also one of the end products of a thousand years of temple architecture, religious symbolism, and ritual construction. For five years truly fabulous discoveries startled public and scholars alike as some seven thousand ritual objects were excavated within the eleven enlargements of the temple situated in the heart of Mexico City. Most of these treasures were obtained from offeratory caches including effigies of deities, ritual masks, sacrificial knives, jade beads, marine animals and seashells, human sacrifices, and major and minor sculptures, which were deposited together with an enormous amount of animal species. Significantly, a large percentage of these objects came from distant regions of the empire as well as the Pacific Ocean and the Gulf of Mexico. The study of this temple will serve as one of the focusing lenses for our vision and understanding of the ways communities, cities, and even empires were organized by a religious cosmovision. And in the Maya areas a series of remarkable excavations at Rio Azul and Tikal are changing the way we understand the purpose and meaning of the pyramids and tombs, which organize much of the Maya ceremonial world.

Another exciting development is the recent decipherment of Maya writing and iconography. The so-called Mysterious Maya of the third to ninth centuries CE achieved an elaborate writing system combining phonetic and ideographic script in inscriptions that covered temples, stairways, reliefs, pictorial manuscripts, stelae (upright stones in ceremonial centers), and vases. Scholars have discovered that the Maya carved vivid narratives showing the powerful interaction of their gods, mythical time, agricultural cycles, dynasties, ancestors, and ritual life in numerous ceremonial centers.

These elaborate narratives, not unlike episodes in a play, show fantastic scenes of bloodletting, descent into the underworld, and the enthronement of royal figures at the cosmic tree. This material shows how the sanctified character of kingship and social stratification played a major role in Mesoamerican religions.

Literary Testimony

In addition to the remains of ceremonial centers and the iconography of the writing systems that survived the conquest, the student is fortunate to have a series of valued translations of selected written documents from the colonial period, including such rich accounts as the *Popul Vuh* or *Book of Council* of the Quiché Maya, Landa's *Relación de las Cosas de Yucatan, The Book of Chilam Balam of Tizimin* of the Yucatan Maya, the *Anales do Cuauhtitlan,* the *Leyenda de los Soles,* the *Codex Cantares Mexicanos,* and the **Florentine Codex** from the Aztec region. Each of these documents, originally written in Quiché Maya or Nahuatl and Spanish (after the conquest), respectively, contain abundant information about the religious symbols and rites, and views of warfare, kingship, and human destiny on earth and in the afterlife as perceived in Aztec and Maya religion. For instance, this passage about the Dual God, Ometeotl, expresses one of the major elements of central Mesoamerican cosmovision:

And the Toltecs knew
that many are the heavens.
They said there are twelve superimposed divisions.
There dwells the true god and his consort.
The celestial god is called the Lord of Duality.
And his consort is called the Lady of Duality, the celestial Lady
which means
he is king, he is Lord, above the twelve heavens.
In the place of sovereignty, in the place of sovereignty, we rule;
my supreme Lord so commands.
Mirror which illumines things.
Now they will join us, now they are prepared.
Drink, drink!
The God of Duality is at work,
Creator of men,
mirror which illumines things.[9]

Here we see two major notions: (1) the organization of the cosmos into thirteen levels (the Dual God occupies the thirteenth); and (2) the division of the cosmos into a dual supernatural reality, male and female, which gives light and understanding (illumines things) to the world.

Of extraordinary value for the study of Maya religion is the *Popul Vuh*, an 8,500-line document containing creation myths, sacred histories, and descriptions of ritual performance, representing a long tradition of Maya religious thought. We see that in Maya mythology the cosmos was created as an extensive ritual performance. "It takes a long performance and account to complete the emergence of all the sky-earth" within a four-quartered world, which was animated through the continual process of "sowing and dawning," that is, planting and harvesting, burial and rebirth, sunset and sunrise. This pattern of planting and rebirth, so vital to the Maya mentality, was also expressed in the periodic rebirth of the cosmos, which passed through four (or six) ages. In the *Popul Vuh* these cycles of repeated cosmic creations and destructions are the setting in which a number of heroes and characters face ordeals and fabulous transformations in journeys through, among other places, **Xibalba,** the Maya underworld. We meet such characters as Heart of Heaven, Crunching Jaguar, Maker of the Blue Green Plate, Blood Woman, Raw Thunderbolt, Plumed Serpent, and the Jaguar Twins, who perpetuated the sowing and dawning of the Maya world through their actions and misdeeds. Study of the postconquest *Popul Vuh* as well as the *Books of Chilam Balam* (books of the Spokesman of the Jaguar), and recent research in contemporary Maya and Mixtec communities herald an awareness that the religious worldviews of the Maya and the Mixtec were not destroyed at the conquest. As we shall see in chapter 5 a number of ritual practices similar to those of the ancient Maya are still carried out today.

The major role played by war and the warrior in the religious worldview of Mesoamerica is richly portrayed in monumental architecture and small sculptured objects as well as pictorial and literary documents. In most parts of Mesoamerican war and the aesthetic, ritual character of the warrior was overtly religious. Great care was given to regulate, through art and aesthetic expression, the profound transformation a human being underwent in training, costuming, combat, victory, defeat, sacrifice, and the afterlife. These actions were guided by a cosmovision saturated with military motifs. For instance the patron deity of the Aztecs, Huitzilopochtli, was the model warrior who, after being magically dressed in his power costume, slew hundreds of enemy deities at the sacred mountain at the center of the world. It was "said that he set men's hearts on fire and gave them courage for war."[10] The religious significance of war in Aztec thought is shown when the birth of this god is immediately followed by his transformation into a ferocious warrior.

Perhaps the richest resource for the study of central Mesoamerican religions is the *Florentine Codex,* a twelve-volume encyclopedic study carried out by the Franciscan priest **Bernardino de Sahagun** within decades after the fall of the Aztec capital. Gods, ceremonies, creation myths, costumes, royalty, animals, medical practices, and the cosmic meaning of the human body are presented in rich and vivid detail. For instance we have many descriptions of how *teotl* (gods, in Nahuatl) and *teotl ixiptla* (human images of gods) were dressed for their ceremonial events. Here is a description of how the *ixiptla* of Xilonen, goddess of the tender maize, was dressed.

> On the tenth day, then the woman (who was the likeness of) Xilonen died. Her face was painted in two colors; she was yellow about her lips, she was chili-red on her forehead. Her paper cap had ears at the four corners; it had quetzal feathers in the form of maize tassels; (she wore) a plaited neck band. Her neck piece consisted of many strings of green stone; a golden disc went over it. (She had) her shift with the water lily (flower and leaf design), and she had her skirt with the water lily (flower and leaf design. She had) her obsidian sandals, her carmine-colored sandals. Her shield and her rattle stick were chili-red. In four directions she entered . . . [11]

In this description we see that the image of the goddess is a living symbol of fertility and powerful objects (obsidian) that, like corn, come out of the earth.

Another important resource combining literary and pictorial information are the Relaciones Geographica, which described political, social, and geographical realities of pre-Hispanic and colonial society. Often, these documents included maps painted in native and colonial styles.

Pictorial Manuscripts

The most beautiful resources for the study of Mesoamerican religions are the eleven surviving preconquest pictorials drawn and painted on bark or deerskin. These colorful documents show that Mesoamerican peoples conceived of *time and space* as thoroughly intertwined. It was the function of ritual life acted out in the ceremonial centers to regulate and restore the detailed interaction of spatial directions, colors, and towns with time periods, anniversaries, births, deaths, journeys, ancestors, and war.

These documents and the sculptured tradition clearly indicate that there were different degrees of writing in Mesoamerican culture, including a spectrum moving from pictorial signs to phonetic scripts. In central Mexico screenfolds and codices show that the cosmological, genealogical, ritual, and historical information was communicated to the community by a combination of pictorial sign and oral interpreter who used images as the basis for verbal presentation. In this way they were storybooks; pictorial books used for the oral description and interpretation of genealogies, town histories, astronomical events, and ritual prescriptions. The pictorial signs and phonetic syllabary depicting the gods, nature, places, kings, warriors, bodily parts, and ritual objects were combined with oral traditions to direct ritual life in all its aspects. This communication of cosmovision and ceremonial life was controlled by the ruling classes.

These documents, plus the remarkable postconquest pictorials (with commentaries in Spanish and sometimes Italian) such as the *Codex Mendoza,* display a powerful obsession with the cycles of agriculture and stars (macrocosmos and microcosmos) and the forces and meaning of sacred time and sacred place. Time was closely observed and each day was considered loaded with celestial and divine influences that determined the inner character and destiny of a person and actions carried out at specific times. This pattern of timekeeping is displayed in the puzzling manuscript called the *Dresden Codex,* a ritual almanac depicting the detailed intimacy of humans, deities, and celestial bodies.

Contemporary Fieldwork Reports

A fourth resource for the study of Mesoamerican religions is contemporary fieldwork carried out in many indigenous communities.

New studies into the calendars, processions, mythology, dream life, healing practices, clothes, market systems, and syncretistic cults reveal both continuities with and changes from the pre-Columbian world.

Given this remarkable ensemble of resources for approaching Mesoamerican religions, what was the religious character of the ancient world of ceremonial centers?

Religion as Worldmaking, Worldcentering, Worldrenewing

As we look at the map of Mesoamerican traditions we see the many locations of different cultures and ceremonial centers. In fact Mesoamerican history was characterized by an eccentric periodicity of creativity, stability, and settlement. The urban tradition was not controlled by one or even several capitals during its distinguished history. Ecological variation and instability as well as intense competition between city-states resulted in periodic collapses of regional capitals, followed by periods of reorganization in which particular ceremonial capitals dominated specific regions. This pattern of order/collapse/recentering/order/collapse and so on was stabilized by certain distinguished periods of creative order. These periods and places of creative order include the Olmecs (1200–300 BCE); Iztapan Culture (300 BCE–100 CE); Classic Maya (200–900 CE); Kaminaljuyu (500 BCE–800 CE); Monte Albán (350–1200 CE): Mixtec (1200–1521 CE); Toltec (1000–1250 CE): and Aztec (1300–1521 CE).

What was the social and religious character of these major periods of cultural integration? In all the cultures listed above three essential processes animated the world of the ceremonial center: worldmaking, worldcentering, and worldrenewing. These processes often interacted to form the religious traditions of Mesoamerican capitals.

Worldmaking

In every case society was organized by and around ceremonial centers modeled on a vision of the structure of the universe. The model of the structure of the universe was contained in the treasured mythology of each community, which told how the world was made and how supernatural forces organized the cosmos.

These ceremonial centers controlled what one scholar has called an **ecological complex** consisting of agricultural production and technological potentials, including art, trading networks, and movements in human population. Each such community, called (in the Aztec world) a *tlatocayotl* (domain of the *tlatoani* or chief speaker), had a ceremonial precinct, often with monumental architecture that served as the ritual theater for acting out the ways in which the world was made and would be remade. Each of the ceremonial centers was a pivot of the universe, acting as a magnet drawing all manner of goods, peoples, and powers into its space.

An example of this magnetic power is described in the sixteenth-century Spanish eyewitness account of Díaz del Castillo:

> To go back to the facts, it seems to me that the circuit of the great pyramid was equal to that of six large town lots, such as they measure in this country, and from below up to where a small tower stood, where they kept their idols, it narrowed . . . There was a report that at the time they began to build that great pyramid, all the inhabitants of that mighty city had placed as offerings in the foundation, gold and silver and pearls and precious stones, and had bathed them with blood of the many Indian prisoners of war who were sacrificed, and had placed there every sort and kind of seed that the land produces, so that their Idols should insure victories and riches, and large crops.[12]

By giving precious offerings to the *axis mundi,* the center of the world of the community, their world got made and remade in terms of agriculture and war.

Perhaps the best example of worldmaking I can use to clarify the term comes from the Aztec myth of the creation of the Fifth Age, the age in which they lived. We are told that before the present world was made, "When no sun had shown and no dawn had broken," the gods gathered in the great ceremonial city of Teotihuacan (Abode of the Gods) to create a new sun. For four days they did penances in the cosmic darkness around a divine fire, which was burning for the duration. Two deities, Nanauatzin (the Pimply One) and Tecuciztecatl (Lord of the Snails) hurled themselves into the fire. The gods sat looking in all directions to see the sun rise. One god, Quetzalcoatl, faced toward the east and there

An artist's reconstruction of the Maya ceremonial center, called the Acropolis, at Copán during the Late Classic period. (From An Album of Maya Architecture *by Tatiana Proskouriakoff. New edition copyright © 1963 by the University of Oklahoma Press.)*

the sun rose. The world was now made. A ceremonial center (Teotihuacan) and a celestial event (sunrise) are linked and aligned uniting heaven and earth. But it was still not centered. The sun was not on its course through the sky, because "when the sun burst forth, he appeared to be red; he kept swaying from side to side." The world has been made with the appearance of the sun, but it had no stability, no process, no center. It has been made through sacrifice, but as we shall see, the world still needed to be centered.

Worldcentering

The cultural world was made and ordered at the ceremonial centers through the creative work of human beings. Human beings acted as the "centering" agents of cultural and religious life in two decisive ways. First, the human body was considered the nexus and unifying structure of the universe. In cosmology, ritual, social structure, and art it is a religious conception of the human body that gives Mesoamerican religions a powerful focus. Second, the world was centered through the work of sacred specialists and royal lineages. Each of these communities operated under the religious authority of an elite corps of priests, rulers, and warriors, who controlled the ritual actions and social groups of farmers, warriors, artists, astronomers, builders, traders, and commoners. This elite community took charge of the goods, peoples, and powers who were drawn into the villages, cities, and capitals and redistributed them according to their own needs. While these leadership groups also insured the well-being of the masses by dispensing food and technology, organizing rituals, and warfare, they made decisive moves to increase their own luxuries and powers in a highly disproportionate way. This led to an extraordinary focus on elite human beings.

Let's return to the myth of the creation of the Fifth Age. How did the cosmos become "centered"? That is, how did it find a pattern, orbit, process? Faced with the threatening condition in which the sun "could only remain still and motionless," the remaining gods committed themselves to a course of action that had a profound influence on the human communities that were created later. One elite god, Ecatl, was chosen to sacrifice *all* the remaining gods to set the sun in motion. Afterward he "arose and exerted himself fiercely and violently as he blew. At once he could move him, who thereupon went on his way" (that is, the sun moved along its orbit). It is through further sacrifice of extraordinary beings that the world becomes centered and regular as the sun moves along its path, dividing time into night and day.

Worldrenewal

The entire style of life of these hierarchical societies was organized by a worldview emphasizing the daily, monthly, and yearly rejuvenation of society and the cosmos. This rejuvenation depended on a complicated range of ritual performances that replayed the myths and images of the origins and transformations of the cosmos and its many parts. These rituals and mythic traditions were not mere repetitions of ancient ways. New rituals and mythic stories were produced to respond to ecological, social, and economic changes and crises. The priests, operating within the sacred confines of their ceremonial centers, used complex calendar systems, divination, and stargazing to direct these extraordinary public rituals to communicate the structure and dynamics of the universe. As we shall see in several upcoming chapters, astronomy played a major role in the calendrical, ritual, and military traditions of Mesoamerica. As with the celestial cycles, so the world of the humans, animals, and plants was renewed constantly within a tight system of ritual displays, pilgrimages, dances, songs, combats, sacrifices, and coronations.

And just as the cosmos was made (sunrise) and centered (sunpath) through sacrifice, so it is renewed through daily, weekly, monthly, and yearly sacrifices of different kinds. These sacrifices take many forms, including bleeding, heart sacrifice, drinking, sexual abstinence, and expending your money on food for the Day of the Dead.

These three major elements of the ceremonial center and celestialevent (worldmaking), human creativity and sacrifice in the hands of an elite (worldcentering), and the commitment to rejuvenation (worldrenewing) will guide the discussion in each of the subsequent chapters. Let us now turn to the history of Mesoamerican religions in order to view its chronology and creative periods.

CHAPTER II

History and Cosmovision in Mesoamerican Religions

And so then they put into words
  the Creation,
  the shaping
  of our first mother and father.
Only yellow corn
and white corn were their bodies.
Only food were the legs
and arms of man.
      Popul Vuh[1]

In many ways Mesoamerica is the most different of the world's early
civilizations. It arose in a land where communication was
exceptionally difficult and natural disaster was frequent; its
occupants had a wealth of domestic plants but few domestic
animals. This meant that not only economics but also the metaphors
of daily life, or of religion and politics, were different from those of
other civilizations: there could neither be "a bull of heaven" nor a
"lamb of God" in ancient Mexico. For all these reasons,
Mesoamerica is a critical case for developing and evaluating general
ideas about world view as a context for understanding the
developing cultural complexity and for the importance of what we
term "religion" in the rise of the first hierarchical polities.
      Henry T. Wright[2]

Where did the peoples and cultures of Mesoamerica originate?
This question has challenged scholar and layperson alike
from the earliest contacts with indigenous American peoples to the
twentieth century. Theologians in the sixteenth century, shocked by
the sudden appearance of masses of peoples never before imagined,
asked, "Are they descendants of Adam and Eve?" Some Europeans,
troubled by how to treat the Indians, wondered, "When Christ died

for the sins of humankind, did he also die for the natives of America?" In anthropological terms Europeans asked, "How do we take people who are scarcely human, or only half human, and teach them to become fully human, as we are?" Central to these questions was the search for the original geographical and cultural homeland of the Aztecs, Mayas, and their ancestors.

Within academic studies it was once thought that native Mesoamericans migrated from Egypt, bringing artistic, political, and religious ideas and symbols with them. The fact that both civilizations produced what appear to be pyramids and hieroglyphics was used to argue that Mesoamerican culture originated in the Old World and traveled to the Americas by various means. Other scholars have argued that they came from Asia, either sailing in *Kon-Tiki*-like boats across the Pacific or gradually migrating down the western coast of America, bringing elements of civilization that served as the basis for the ceremonial centers, calendars, and rituals of the Mayas and Aztecs. Recently some scholars have argued that Asian cultures strongly influenced the Costa Rican area of Mesoamerica, bringing Buddhist artistic and theological traditions to the New World three thousand years ago. This type of approach, called the diffusionist approach, argues that the great civilizations of the Americas were developed by migrating peoples who left original centers of cultures and transplanted the roots of civilization (monumental architecture, writing, calendrics) in American soil. This approach is largely based on a series of similarities (pyramids, art motifs, toys, cotton) found in Cambodia, India, China, and the Americas.

One extreme example of diffusionist thought very popular in the nineteenth century claimed that the lost continent of Atlantis or Mu was the original home of ancient American civilizations. Using Plato's description of the sinking of the legendary continent of Atlantis, proponents of the submerged continent theory argued that the aboriginal Americans saved themselves in the nick of time and brought to America their great civilization. An English nobleman, Lord Kingsborough, spent much of his family fortune trying to demonstrate that the native inhabitants of Mesoamerica were the descendants of the thirteen lost tribes of Israel. Perhaps the most fantastic formulation, popular in the twentieth century, is Erik von Daniken's claim that ancient astronauts brought the genius of extraterrestrial civilizations to ancient Mesoamerica. The theory of cultural diffusion raises many interesting questions for the researcher interested in tracing the history of ancient transportation and communication patterns. But similarities in cultures do not demonstrate close or significant contact. This is especially the case when we realize that not a single object from Asian cultures has been discovered in the Americas. And many objects vital in Old World culture, such as the wheel, the cart, the plough, iron, and stringed instruments, are missing in the pre-Columbian New World.

In the case of the Americas such ridiculous formulations as von Daniken's, Kingsborough's, and some others may conceal a powerful ethnocentric bias. The implication of some diffusionist interpretations is that Native Americans were not capable of achieving extraordinary levels of cultural creativity on their own but needed the stimulus and remnants of superior foreigners to become civilized.

Scholars have clearly shown that Mesoamerican civilizations, in fact all New World civilizations and cultures, *developed as a result of cultural creativity indigenous to the Americas.* This is not to deny that impressive similarities between Old and New World cultures exist. Monumental architectural structures, which we refer to as pyramids, existed in Egypt, Indonesia, Mexico, Guatemala, and other parts of Mesoamerica. But the so-called pyramids of Mesoamerica were actually huge platforms constructed to support temples, which together served as theatrical stages upon which were acted out the pomp, cosmovision, and political spectacles of the city. It is true that some Mesoamerican pyramid/temples served (as in the case' of Egypt) as royal tombs and monuments to ancestors, but it is more likely that they were primarily places of public performance of religious ceremonies linking the living and the dead in a day-to-day fashion. Also, in Mesoamerica, specific pyramid/temples could be utilized by *successive rulers* for exterior displays of cosmovision and politics as well as for interior burials of individuals and treasure.

Another major difference between the monumental cities of the Old and New Worlds was the intricate and widespread 260-day ritual calendar so influential among many Mesoamerican peoples. Although it appears that limited contact between Asian cultures and the peoples of Mesoamerica took place, the Olmecs, Huastecs, Mayas, Tlaxcalans, Toltecs, Mixtecs, Otomis, Aztecs, and all other indigenous cultures developed their own cultural processes independent of significant contributions from outside civilizations. These cultural processes were concentrated and crystallized in the numerous ceremonial centers, city-states, and cosmovisions that organized Mesoamerican society.

In this chapter we will present an overview of the history of Mesoamerican religions from two points of view. We will describe the patterns of worldmaking, worldcentering, and worldrenewing in chronological order beginning with the rise of agriculture, proceeding through the three major stages of historical development called the Formative Period (1800 BCE–200 CE), the Classic Period (200–900 CE), and the Post-Classic Period (900–1500 CE). And we will also emphasize the creative moments and major contributions to the formation of Mesoamerican religions.

Plants and the Sacred Dead

Mesoamerica was a geographical and cultural area covering the southern two-thirds of Mexico and significant portions of Central America. In this extensive region human populations developed intensive agricultures, which served as the partial basis for the rise of urban civilizations. It is evident that human populations from northeast Asia (groups of Mongoloid peoples) entered the New World as early as 50,000 BCE and as late as the time of Christ over and along the Bering Strait land bridge that connected Siberia and Alaska. These hunting and gathering peoples migrated southward and eventually reached the Basin of Mexico by 20,000 BCE. They carried a circumpolar and circumboreal hunting culture into the Americas, which included shamanism and ceremonial ties to animals and their spirits. Various human physical types speaking many languages migrated into North America and Mesoamerica; over 250 languages for the area covering Mexico and Guatemala have been identified.

As these peoples moved into Mesoamerica, they encountered a geography of contrasts and wonders, highlands and lowlands, with an astonishing variety of ecosystems. High mountain ranges, periodically volcanic, form high valley systems and plateaus where major cultural centers developed at different periods in history. These high, mountainous areas sweep down on the eastern and western sides into lowland areas that give way to the Gulf of Mexico, the Caribbean Sea, and the Pacific Ocean. One writer has compared sections of Mesoamerica to the shape of a pyramid with temples and open spaces on top. The plateaus and high valleys as well as the fertile areas of the lowlands served as important centers of pre-Hispanic cultures.

The most creative cultural event in the pre-urban history of Mesoamerica was the control of food energy contained in plants. As the quotation that begins this chapter indicates, the natives compared the creation of human life with the creation of corn: The substance of the human body consisted of yellow and white corn! The domestication of agriculture, fundamental to the eventual rise of permanent villages, ceremonial centers, and social differentiation developed slowly between 6500 BCE and 2000 BCE as peoples learned to plant and harvest corn, beans, squash, avocados, cotton, and chilies. All of these plants were perceived as imbued with sacred powers and came to play important roles in the mythology, calendar, ritual, costumes, ancestor worship, and performances of Mesoamerican religions. Centuries later, in the Aztec capital of Tenochtitlan, corn was one of the rewards for the good citizen who acted diligently. In the ceremony Teotleco (The Gods Arrive) the ritual begins when a priest provided

> a small basket of dried grains of maize, or else four ears of maize: in some places, three ears of maize; if [the householders] were very poor, it was two ears of maize that he gave them. . . . And no one just idly ate the maize toasted on the embers; only those who were diligent, acceptable, careful, wakeful, who trusted not too much their own diligence.[3]

Archaeologists have discerned that during the last part of these agricultural periods people developed some of the ritual relationships to the human body that eventually became central to the religions of numerous Mesoamerican peoples. These included shamanism, special offerings to the dead, the dismemberment of human beings, sacrifice, and cremation. Cultures practiced rituals dedicated to the hunting and restoration of animals and their spirits as well as to the planting, fertilization, and harvesting of plants. It appears that some powerful beliefs in the longevity of the human spirit and an afterlife were present. Some humans were buried with companions whose involuntary death provided assistance to the leader or master in the world of supernatural entities. Around 2500 BCE multiple forms of ritual and domestic pottery, including cooking utensils, clay figurines of women, animals, and deities, were developed in central Mexico; and by 1800 BCE the stage was set for what Eric Wolf called "villages and holy towns," in which some of the basic cultural religious patterns for the next three thousand years were established.

The subsequent period of cultural history has been designated by historians as the Formative Period (see Chronology). Between 1800 BCE and 200 CE cultures began to form permanent ceremonial centers containing impressive monumental, ceremonial architecture including pyramids, palaces, tombs, and spacious outdoor ritual precincts. It was within these sacred precincts, examples of what we have called worldmaking, that ritual performances were acted out and directed by priestly elites who managed the integration of economic, political, artistic, astronomical, and spiritual forces. One pervasive performance was ritual dancing in community ceremonial centers. Archaeologists working in Oaxaca, Mexico, have uncovered figurines depicting dance societies as well as conch-shell trumpets and turtle-shell drums dating from 1200 BCE to 600 BCE. The dancers are dressed as fantastic animals and as jaguars, birds, and pumas reflecting the sacralization of human-animal relationship. Dance societies dressed in these animal motifs were active when the Spaniards arrived and are still performing in indigenous communities and for tourists today.

It is also apparent that important private and public ceremonies of ritual bloodletting were carried out. We know that in the Classic (200–900 CE) and Post-Classic (900–1500 CE) periods priests drew blood from tongues, earlobes, thighs, and sexual organs using fish spines, maguey thorns, obsidian blades, or, in the case of Mayan lords, knotted strings of thorns. Some of these bloodletting instruments have been found in ruins of private households of public ceremonial precincts in Oaxaca between 1200 BCE and 600 BCE. These discoveries indicate that ceremonial centers were within domestic dwellings as well as in the larger community spaces.[4]

It is also important that a number of public ceremonial buildings in the Oaxaca region share astronomical orientations (that is, they are aligned toward horizon points where sun, moon, Venus, or other celestial bodies appear) with ceremonial structures hundreds of miles away. This indicates a shared cosmovision that influenced ceremonial architecture and ritual very early in Mesoamerican history. This combination of ceremonial center (microcosmos) and astronomical event (macrocosmos) is what helps create order in the world.

The art and architecture of the earliest Mesoamerican civilization, called the Olmecs by archaeologists, shows that religious ideas and symbols were not only mental activities, but rather tied up with daily work, trade, social order, and warfare.

The Olmec World: Jaguars and Giants in Stone

One of the real challenges for students of religion in general and Mesoamerica in particular is to understand cultures that did not produce what we consider writing. Many Mesoamerican cultures were primarily oral in their modes of expression. Others, such as the Mixtec, the Maya, and the Aztec, produced pictorial systems with varying degrees of symbolic expressions including pictograms, ideograms, and phonetic script. The range of expression in Mesoamerica is so complex and varied that it has challenged scholars to rethink the category of "writing" and to reevaluate the status of cultural superiority that has too long accompanied it.

In addition to the important task of interpreting oral traditions, we are often faced with the need to work with "mute texts"— stones, sacred stones, ceremonial architecture, pottery, and even human and animal bones. The most vivid example of this situation is the Olmec culture (Olmec means "people from the land of the rubber trees"), whose scattered ceremonial centers took shape around 1800 BCE and collapsed by 300 BCE. The name Olmec was used by an indigenous group living in this area at the time of the conquest. It is not known what the ancient community called itself.

The social history of permanent Mesoamerican ceremonial centers begins around 1800 BCE with the rise of the **Olmec Style** of art and architecture found in a variety of sacred precincts and caves, originating in the lowland regions of southern Vera Cruz and western Tabasco near the coast of the Gulf of Mexico. This region is one of the richest archaeological zones in the world, probably having the highest density of sites per square mile in all of

One of many colossal basalt heads carved by the Olmecs at ceremonial centers on Mexico's gulf coast. This monolith is nearly three meters in height and was transported over fifty miles from its quarry site. Monument 1 from San Lorenzo, c. 1200 BCE. (Photograph courtesy of Michael Coe.)

Mesoamerica. Called the "Mother Culture" of later Mesoamerican civilizations by the Mexican artist and scholar Miguel Covarrubias, the Olmecs set in motion certain religious patterns that were elaborated and developed by later peoples. Evidence of these patterns is found in a glorious tradition of stone carvings, rock paintings, and religious imagery for us to admire and interpret.

The most impressive pattern of Olmec culture was the manner in which the earth was reshaped as a means of religious expression. The Olmec media for art and symbolic expression were jade, ba-

This stone carving depicts a person seated in a stylized cave, symbolizing the earth-monster. The emerging scroll represents wind or the sound of thunder, while precious raindrops, representing fertility, fall from the clouds. Monument 1 El-Rey, Chalcatzingo, Morelos, Mexico c. 600 BCE. (Courtesy of Michael Coe.)

salt, clay, and the earth itself in the forms of caves, hills, and artificial volcanoes such as was used at La Venta to represent an earth pyramid. Each of these media was transformed to represent the realities of social hierarchy and religious imagination. Caves became the setting for cave paintings and rituals of mythic events while cliffs became the place of carvings of human-animal-spirit relations. The ceremonial centers were assemblages of sacred spaces made of redesigned earthly materials arranged on and *within* the earth. This tie to the earth is reflected in Olmec mythology expressing themes of emergence from caves, human-jaguar transformation, and the relations of animals to rulers. We can see the tissues of nature-human relations in the bas relief from Chalcatzingo where an Olmec ruler or man-god is seated in a cave holding a box surrounded by clouds, water, jade (circular motifs), vegetation, and the stone representing the earth itself. And in at least one case, archaeologists have found large mosaics layed out to form a jaguar mask buried in multiple layers beneath the surface of the earth.

The Olmec heartland of the coastal region has been compared to the "fertile crescent" of Mesopotamia due to its extraordinary potential for corn farming and its rich supply of fish, aquatic birds, frogs, and toads. In this region of abundant natural resources the Olmecs built permanent ceremonial centers accompanied by an alluring art style appearing in jade miniatures, pottery, stelae (upright standing stones with carved imagery), and large sculpture. The culture managed to spread its religious political and artistic conceptions up into the central Mexican highlands, into the western lowlands, and as far south as El Salvador through the control of long-distance trade routes and exploration.

Although we cannot tell if the Olmecs achieved territorial control over large parts of Mesoamerica, it is clear that their artistic and conceptual style was spread far and wide. This style included the ritual calendar and ritual burials, and a profound relationship with animals whose visages permeate their art. In fact Olmec ceremonial centers were ornamented with a number of fantastic religious motifs depicting animal-human relations. Such combinations as human-jaguar, jaguar-bird, bird-jaguar-caiman (alligator), jaguar-caiman-fish, and caiman-human appear in different sites. Rattlesnakes, fer-de-lances, harpy eagles, and monkeys were also considered manifestations of the sacred sky, earth, and underworld. It is possible that these carefully carved, sometimes precious stone images reflect the belief in spirit helpers who took the form of powerful, aggressive, even dangerous animals serving in the practice of shamans. We know from later Maya and Aztec periods that real and fantastic animals or entities became intimately associated with all individuals. They could function as the spiritual guides of sacred specialists, warriors, priests, and the ruling class.

One site that depicts early conceptions of Mesoamerican deities was San Lorenzo, which was fully formed by 1200 BCE. It was suddenly destroyed around 900 BCE, when many of its religious and historical images were mutilated and buried. In addition to the over two hundred ceremonial mounds identified at this site, the most astonishing discovery was the six colossal stone heads carved with powerful simplicity depicting individual human faces with mongoloid features, each wearing a helmet like headgear. Up to nine feet in height, weighing 40 tons, these heads, along with a number of other huge stone monuments, are carved from rocks in the Tuxtla mountains over 45 miles from the site. Their transportation to San Lorenzo over land and water, as well as their artistic sophistication, reflects both a complex level of social organization and a deep concern for religious symbolism. It is difficult to understand the meaning of these giant stone heads, which were in some cases lined up at the edge of a ceremonial area. It has been suggested that they represent the heads of dead warriors or portraits of rulers, whose images guarded the sacred precincts from invaders. It is likely that they represent the Olmec concern with royal genealogy by memorializing rulers who appear as gigantic beings influencing daily life.

Another impressive site is the ceremonial center of **La Venta,** where jaguar motifs and giant heads sculpted in stone embroider a small, swampy, stoneless island. In the heart of this carefully planned site stands Mesoamerica's first great pyramid. It is a fluted, cone-shaped natural structure 420 feet in diameter and 100 feet high, with its outward surface consisting of alternating rises and depressions that give it the appearance of a volcano. Nearby, archaeologists found the buried remains of two juveniles heavily covered with thick cinnabar pigment accompanied by offerings of jade beads and stingray spines. This ceremonious concern for the dead buried near the heart of the sacred precinct shows a special relation between certain human groups and the *axis mundi*. This combination of human and temple at the heart of a settlement indicates the early pattern of what we have called worldcentering. In a number of later cultures the royal dead were buried in tombs within the sacred precincts, suggesting a special relation between sacred space, ceremonial structures, the earth, the dead, and the underworld. A number of other spectacular caches, perhaps offerings to the gods, containing jade, jaguar mosaics, and pierced concave mirrors made of iron ore, were excavated at La Venta.

One of the greatest religious achievements of Mesoamerica was the invention of a ritual calendar of extraordinary accuracy. At a third major site, Tres Zapotes, all of the Olmec artistic and religious characteristics, plus one, were combined in the sacred center. The most famous monument of Tres Zapotes is called stela C. It contains a jaguar monster mask on one side and a column of bars and dot numerals on the other. However, it has been determined that this is a post-Olmec monument containing bars and dots that have been deciphered as the date 31 BCE. The suggestion is that the Olmec and not the Maya, as previously thought, invented, toward the end of their history, the great calendar system called the **long count,** which was instrumental in organizing ritual and social life in parts of Mesoamerica.

Astronomy and the Sacred Ball Game

One of the most intriguing types of ceremonial centers was the sacred ball court (*tlachco*) in Nahuatl, *Pok-ta-pok* in Maya) where the ball game was played. Spread throughout Mesoamerica, this ritual tradition has one of its most impressive expressions at the site of El Tajin in modern-day Vera Cruz, where it was developed as a major cosmic symbol between 200 CE and 500 CE. Typically the game was played on a ball court laid out like a capital letter I with a central narrow gallery or playing court leading at both ends to short perpendicular spaces. This was a stylized representation of the four-quartered universe joined by the central or fifth region. The court and the game constituted a cosmogram (image of the cosmos) and religious drama. Detailed carvings of the ball game ritual from El Tajin show the dress, action, and religious meaning of this game. It appeared that on certain occasions the losing warriors, or at least a representative, was publicly and ritually sacrificed and beheaded in the shrine.

Later, in Aztec times, it appears that the playing court represented the narrow passageway of the underworld through which the sun traveled at night. The game represented a cosmic struggle between competing factions to see which group could bring the sun out of the underworld by hitting the ball through one of the two perforated rings on the sides of the court. The ball court, then, is a kind of temple in which the solar drama is acted out in human time and space. The sacrifice of the losing player may represent the offering of energy in the form of blood and human life in order to give birth to the new sun.

Fortunately the Dominican priest Diego Durán, who lived in New Spain between 1545 and 1588, asked his native parishioners about the native ball game. He wrote,

> So that we can understand its form and begin to appreciate the skill and dexterity with which this game was played, it must be noted that ball courts existed in all the illustrious, civilized, and powerful

cities and towns, in those ruled by either the community or the lords, the latter stressing [the game] inordinately. A regular competition existed between the two [types of communities]. [The ball courts] were enclosed with ornate and handsomely carved walls. The interior floor was of stucco, finely polished and decorated with figures of the god and demons to whom the game was dedicated and whom the players held to be their patrons in that sport. These ball courts were larger in some places than in others.

Durán describes the walls, sculptures, and crowds this way:

The height of the wall was anywhere between eight and eleven feet high, running all around [the court]. Because of heathen custom, around [the wall] were planted wild palms or trees which give red seeds, whose wood is soft and light. Crucifixes and carved images are made of it today. The surrounding walls were adorned with merlons or stone statues, all spaced out. [These places] became filled to bursting when there was a game of all the lords, when warlike activities ceased, owing to truces or other causes, thus permitting [the games].[5]

Two other important religious innovations, astronomical alignments and pictorial narratives, took place by the time the ceremonial centers of Monte Albán (600–300 BCE) and Izapa (200 BCE–100 CE) were formed. At the heart of over two hundred permanent sites near the present-day city of Oaxaca in southern Mexico stood the elaborately built Zapotec hilltop center of Monte Albán. It consisted of temples, courtyards, ball courts, and tombs for elites scattered throughout the site. Among its many characteristics are the alignment of buildings with particular astronomical events plus the appearance of writing and the elaboration of the long count calendar system. Several buildings were built so as to face a particular horizon appearance of a celestial body or a constellation. This relationship of the orientation of ceremonial buildings to astronomical events such as the solstices, equinoxes, and Venus cycles is of major importance in our understanding of cosmovision. It shows that early in the architectural record Mesoamericans were expressing the conviction that human and cultural spaces (such as homes, pyramids, temples, ball courts) had to be in tune or aligned with celestial bodies and their patterns. This integration of sky and earth and human society in Mesoamerica has been intensely studied by archaeoastronomers such as Anthony Aveni who has

A ceremonial ball court of the Late Classic Maya site of Copan, in Honduras.
(Courtesy of Linda Schele, photographer.)

shown that in some cases ceremonial buildings were constructed to mark the passage of Venus from its first to its last appearance in the Venus cycle, above the horizon. We will see more of this relationship of stargazing and temple alignment in later cultures.

Recently archaeologists have realized that Iztapa, in Guatemala, which contained over seventy-five pyramid mounds and a large number of stone stelae, was a major transition point between the Olmec style and the Maya achievement. Of particular importance are the pictorial narratives, stories carved in stone depicting human and celestial forces. We see humans and deities involved in battles, sacrifices (including decapitation), and rituals, all associated with a stylized sacred world tree. Many of these religious ideas and actions were to find their most brilliant expression among the Classic Maya, who now entered the stage.

The Classic Maya: Kings and Cosmic Trees

The astonishing achievements of the Classic Maya civilization have inspired awe and admiration in all who come to study them. A number of religious innovations appear to crystallize in Maya society between 200 CE and 900 CE, a period designated as the Classic Maya. Among the major elements of the Maya achievement were the mathematically ingenious calendar; lavishly decorated ceremonial centers; a heightened conception of the royal person; writing; and a complex mythology of the underworld and cosmic regeneration. It is also amazing that these city-states and achievements developed in the forests and jungle environments, where civilizations have usually had a difficult time taking hold. Called the "Mysterious Maya" for generations, they were once believed to have been a peace-loving civilization of stargazing priests whose theological vision should be imitated by modern people. Recent studies have revealed a more typical civilization motivated by warfare, the desire to dominate, hierarchies, elaborate ceremonies associated with lineage and ancestors and complex esoteric religious ideas. One of the greatest mysteries about the Classic Mayas is the **Maya collapse:** the rapid and near total collapse of many of their ceremonial centers during the short period of 830 CE to 930 CE. It appears that a pervasive series of crises shattered the Maya world, stimulated by interlocking collapses in the agricultural, ceremonial, and political systems that held the society together.

The character of the Classic Maya world is well represented in a small jade plaque discovered in 1864 by workmen digging a canal in eastern Guatemala. Called the Leiden Plate because eventually it was taken to Leiden, Holland, this 8½-inch object contains two typical images of Maya life. On one side we find a long count calendar date corresponding to 320 CE, while on the other side we see an extravagantly dressed Maya lord stepping on a midget-sized captive cowering underneath him. This combination of sacred time, warfare, and social hierarchy carved in fine jade illustrates the integration of vital elements of the Maya achievement.

One of the most creative religious achievements of the Classic Maya was the long count calendar. Although this calendric system had earlier origins based on intense astronomical observations, it was the Maya who elaborated the cosmological conviction that human life would be most favorable if it mirrored the mathematically expressible cycles of the heavens. As a means of recording important human events and attuning human order to the celestial order, the Maya developed a calendar system with many different counts

This painted wall depicts the arraignment of prisoners by a victorious procession of elites and warriors. The prisoners are being tortured by having their fingernails plucked before their final sacrifice. Structure 1, Room 2, Bonampak, Chiapas, Mexico, 8th century CE. *(Photograph courtesy of the Peabody Museum, Harvard University. Photograph by F. P. Orchard.)*

including the Tzolkin (260-day count related to human gestation), the Haab (365-day count related to solar cycle), the Long Count (related to ancestor worship and lineages), the calendar round (a 52-year cycle), the Lords of the Night (nine-day interval), and the lunar cycle. The largest count in this system was the Long Count, which measured each day from the beginning date of the present cosmic era in 3114 BCE and prophesied its end on December 23, 2012. Each day was measured by a system of five subunits and enabled the priest to compute dates in colossal cycles going back to at least nine million years BCE as marked on inscriptions in several ceremonial centers.[6] Mathematicians have pointed out that an understanding of the concept zero is necessary for such computations. The Maya marked these days so they could be in conscious contact with the sacred forces appearing in the terrestrial world at carefully determined intervals. Unfortunately this calendar system largely faded from use, excerpt in scattered parts of Yucatan, after the Classic Maya society collapsed.

The social style of this universe appears in the murals of **Bon-ampak** ("city of painted walls"), which were discovered by accident in 1948. A photographer following a jungle deer saw it go into a small temple barely visible in the overgrowth. Once within he was surprised to find murals covering the walls and ceilings of three rooms depicting the formal aspects of Maya court life and a series of scenes of bloodletting, warfare, human sacrifice, ceremonial processions, and dances on pyramids, all surrounded by astronomical and calendrical signs. In one alluring scene a procession of deity impersonators dressed as animals (crocodiles, crabs, jaguars) accompany a musical ensemble preparing to process.

During this long period of cultural creativity the Maya elaborated a profound religious cosmovision based on the "symbolism of the center." The Maya believed the world was centered by a combination of the sacred flowering cosmic tree and the royal person (**Mah K'ina,** great sun lord), both linked to the world of ancestors. This cosmovision is made clearest at the beautiful site of Palenque, where pictorial programs, carved on a series of ceremonial temples and buildings, show how the royal families ruled, communicated with gods, died, and passed power from the dead to the living and rejuvenated the agricultural world. As we shall see in chapter 4, the Maya lords had a grandiose conception of their role in sacred history. Let us now move over 400 miles to the north where the imperial capital of Teotihuacan was constructed.

Teotihuacan: The Imperial Capital

The most frequently visited archaeological site in the Americas is Teotihuacan, known to most people as the "pyramids." Located in the central highlands 30 miles northeast of present-day Mexico City, Teotihuacan (as known to the Aztecs five hundred years after the city collapsed) means "the place where one becomes deified." Not only did it contain monumental architecture, but it was also designed as a gigantic image of the cosmos. At its peak, around 500 CE, Teotihuacan was populated by over 200,000 people who shared in the prestige of a capital that influenced many cities and towns within and beyond the central plateau of Mexico.

Surprisingly, Teotihuacan had its beginnings in a cave. This greatest of Classic cities, with its immense towering pyramids of the sun and moon, elaborate ceremonial courtyards, and residential palaces (the city contains over seventy-five temples), originated underground at the mouth of a well. Recent excavations show that directly under the Pyramid of the Sun lie the remains of an ancient tunnel and shrine area, which was an early, if not the original, sacred center for ritual and perhaps the goal of pilgrimages. Throughout Mesoamerican history caves are valued as the place of origins of ancestral peoples and the openings to the powers and gods of the underworld. Like the city that was to spread out above it, this cave was artificially reshaped and decorated into the form of a four-petaled flower. In some of the later paintings and pictorial narratives the Mesoamerican cosmos is symbolized by a four-petaled flower representing the division of space into four cardinal regions around a center. It is possible that the cave was Teotihuacan's earliest *imago mundi,* or sacred image of the cosmos.

The entire city of Teotihuacan was laid out by its planners and architects as a four-part imitation of the cosmos. In this way it was not only a container of religious symbolism, it was itself a religious symbol. The city's hundreds of residential, ritual, and craft buildings followed a grid pattern that was organized by two main avenues: the Street of the Dead (over 2,000 meters long) and the East West Avenue, which crossed at right angles in the center of the city dividing it into four huge quadrants. It is important to note that a number of natural features such as creeks and hills were altered to conform to this scheme.

This layout had clear linkages to astronomical events. The great stairway of the Pyramid of the Sun, for example, faces a westerly point on the horizon where the **Pleiades,** called Tianquitzli, meaning "marketplace" (or Miec meaning "heap") by later Nahuatl peoples, sat directly in front of it. What exact religious moment in the city's calendar this day signified may never be clear; but it is obvious that there was a noble attempt to achieve a harmony, and to express that harmony publicly between the great pyramid and celestial patterns. This is also demonstrated by the fact that the Pleiades made its first yearly appearance above the horizon before the sun rose on the day it passed through the zenith. It

The Pyramid of the Sun at Teotihuacan. This monumental structure dominated the ceremonial center and imperial capital of the Valley of Mexico from CE 200 until CE 750. In the foreground are platforms along the Street of the Dead that supported other smaller temples and dwellings. At the height of its urban expansion (300–600 CE), Teotihuacan rivaled the most populated of Old World cities. (Photograph courtesy of Lawrence G. Desmond.)

is likely that these two stellar events, key to the cosmovision of so many Mesoamerican cultures, signaled the moment when the elites organized the masses of people to ritually prepare for the new agricultural season.

The art of Teotihuacan also reveals an abundance of cults dedicated to the activities of warfare, titular deities, fertility, ball games, dynastic rulers and burials. The earlier evidence of these religious themes that we have studied now takes center stage in the evidence at Teotihuacan. And although we have no written material and very limited oral tradition directly related to Teotihuacan, it appears that deities which in later cultures are identified as Quetzalcoatl (the Feathered Serpent), **Tlaloc** (the Rain God), Xipe Totec (the God of Vegetation), and Xochiquetzal (the Goddess of Sexuality) were highly revered in the great capital.

It is clear that later cultures, especially the Aztecs, looked to Teotihuacan as the Place of Origins. They claimed in their sacred history that the Fifth Sun, the Aztec Era, was born out of sacrificial fire in the great city at the beginning of time. The story of the creation of the Fifth Age of the cosmos, the age of the Aztecs begins:

> It is told that when yet [all] was in darkness, when yet no sun had shown and no dawn had broken—it is said—the gods gathered themselves there at Teotihuacan. They spoke . . . "Who will take it upon himself to be the sun, to bring the dawn?"[7]

Teotihuacan's monumental magnificence, precise spatial order, exuberant craft and market systems, and sacred prestige helped make this city the center of an expanding, pulsating empire. Although its position of absolute dominance over many other cities appears to have lasted for less than two hundred years, its status as the center for this region of the Mesoamerican world cannot be limited to the time when its art styles were imitated. For Teotihuacan was the first true capital, the first great place in central Mexico, where a fully integrated, rich, and well-fed society operated under the authority of supernatural forces and cosmo-magical formulas.

Tollan: City of the Plumed Serpent

> Quetzalcoatl was looked upon as a god. He was worshiped and prayed to in former times in Tollan, and there his temple stood: very high, very tall. Extremely tall, extremely high.[8]

This passage, recited by an Aztec elder to the Spanish priest-researcher Bernardino de Sahagun, refers to one of the most creative periods of the history of Mesoamerican religions, namely the Toltec empire. In Aztec times (1325–1521 CE) young people were educated about the cultural brilliance and religious genius of the ancient kingdom of Tollan (Place of Reeds) ruled by the priest-king **Topiltzin Quetzalcoatl** (Our Young Prince the Plumed Serpent), who was a devotee of the great god Quetzalcoatl. Following the rapid eighth-century collapse of Teotihuacan as the center of the Mesoamerican world, the "Great Tollan" was formed, consisting of over twenty sizable settlements surrounding the capital of Tollan, also called Tula. According to the sacred history taught in Aztec *calmecacs* or schools, Tollan existed in a golden age where agricultural abundance, technological excellence, artistic perfection, and spiritual genius were united under the patronage of the great divine being, Quetzalcoatl, the Plumed Serpent. Tollan was inhabited by the legendary Toltecs, whose very name signified artistic excellence. They were remembered as

> very wise. Their works were all good, all perfect, all wonderful, all miraculous, their houses beautiful, tiled in mosaics, smooth stuccoed, very marvelous.[9]

In this setting of cultural genius and economic stability, the Toltecs invented the calendar,

> originated the year count, they established the way in which the night, the day would work . . . they discerned the orbits of the stars . . .[10]

and invented rituals of divination. Of course we have already seen that many of these cultural forms were invented and developed a millennium before the Toltecs. But with the rapid collapse of earlier cultures these traditions were periodically reinvented and developed. Also, in Aztec times, all societies seeking prestige claimed their descent from the Toltec lineage.

All this abundance and creativity was organized by a ceremonial center consisting of a great pyramid surrounded by four temples, beautifully decorated, facing the four cardinal points of the universe. At the center of this world lived the priest-king Quetzalcoatl, who had fabulous powers endowed upon him by his god. It was recited in the Aztec schools, "Truly with him it began, truly from him it flowed out, from Quetzalcoatl—all art and knowledge."

Scholars have worked diligently through the pictorial, architectural, and ethnohistorical evidence to discover that there were at least two Quetzalcoatls. One, a powerful creator god, was one of the four children of the divine duality, **Ometeotl,** who dwelled in the innermost part of heaven, above the twelfth level. In different accounts Quetzalcoatl creates the cosmos, recovers the ancestral bones from the underworld (**Mictlan**), and acquires corn from the **Mountain of Sustenance** for humans. The other was his human representative or *hombre-dios* (man-god) who ruled Tollan and brought it to its apex of greatness. The human Quetzalcoatl was

also known by his calendrical name as Ce Acatl Topiltzin Quetzalcoatl (One Reed, Our Young Prince the Plumed Serpent). He was
remembered in song, poetry, and art as having a miraculous birth,
a rigorous training for the priesthood that included mountain
asceticism, a fierce career as a warrior, and a brief period as a triumphant king. During his kingship he apparently attempted a religious revolution. According to one source Topiltzin Quetzalcoatl
changed the ritual tradition of sacrificing human beings and substi-
tuted quail, butterflies, and rabbits. This radical departure provoked the magical attacks of his archrival Tezcatlipoca, Lord of the
Smoking Mirror, whose sacrificial cults drove Topiltzin Quetzalcoatl into exile. In one surviving tradition it was believed that the
fleeing prince might return in a future calendar round in the year *ce
acatl* or One Reed. One Reed also corresponded to the year 1519,
when the Spaniards arrived in Mexico; and Cortés was believed,
for a time, to be the return of Quetzalcoatl's power. Around the
eleventh century Tollan, like the Maya and the culture of Teotihuacan, fell into rapid ruin, perhaps as a result of Quetzalcoatl's
defeat. But the Toltec tradition lived on and was to become one of
the keys to the rise of the warrior religion of the Aztecs.

Aztec War, Cosmic Conflict

A fragment of Aztec poetry reads like a combination of cosmic security and military boast.

> Proud of Itself
> Is the city of Mexico-Tenochtitlan
> Here no one fears to die in war
> This is our glory
> This is your Command
> Oh Giver of Life
> Have this in mind, oh princes
> Who could conquer Tenochtitlan?
> Who could shake the foundation of heaven?[11]

Four elements in this verse guide our historical overview of Aztec religion: warfare; the concentration of order within the capital
of Tenochtitlan; a fear of cosmic instability; and a connection to
the intentions of the gods. In fact the formation of Aztec religion

was accomplished in the capital city of Tenochtitlan, located in the central valley of Mexico between the fourteenth and sixteenth centuries CE. The Aztec religious tradition combined and transformed a number of ritual, mythic, and cosmological elements from the heterogeneous cultural groups, including the Toltecs, who inhabited the central plateau of Mesoamerica.

When the Aztec precursors, the **Chichimecas** (*chichi,* dog, and *mecatl,* rope, lineage), migrated into the lake region (there were five interconnected lakes covering the valley floor) in the thirteenth century, the valley was organized by warring city-states constantly competing for land and tribute payments of food, luxuries, and military prisoners. This fragmented world was partly the result of the twelfth-century collapse of the Toltec empire. The Toltec collapse brought waves of Chichimecas and Toltec remnants into the Valley of Mexico, where they interacted with different city-states and religious traditions in periodic and intense conflict. One Chichimec group, who called themselves the Mexica, settled on a swampy island in the middle of the lakes and within a hundred years organized a ferocious military and political unit with the capacity of dominating by force and persuasion an increasing number of city-states in central Mexico. They achieved dominance during the revolution of 1424–1426 against the ruling capital of the Tepanec empire, Azcapotzalco. Along with two other rebelling city-states, Tlacopan and Texcoco, they formed the feared Triple Alliance; but it was the Aztecs of Tenochtitlan who assumed supreme power in central Mesoamerica. They did this through the control of trade routes, an aggressive cosmovision, and large-scale military campaigns that were celebrated in the lavish rituals held in the various ceremonial centers of the capital.

Seldom has a capital city fit the category of "center of the world" more completely than Tenochtitlan. While the high plateau of Mexico was roughly the center of Mesoamerica, the Valley of Mexico was the heart of the plateau; interconnected lakes formed the center of the valley and Tenochtitlan was constructed near the center of the lakes. From the beginning of the Common Era, when the great imperial capital of Teotihuacan was organized into four great quarters around a massive ceremonial center 30 miles to the north of the valley of Mexico, the central highlands had been the dominant cultural region of central Mesoamerica.

Even though Mesoamerican civilization was periodically fragmented, its reintegration was controlled, at least in the cultural regions north of the Maya regions, by cities located at the top of the geographical pyramid. Between 1300 and 1521 all roads of central Mesoamerica led into the lake region of the valley from which the magnificent capital of the Aztecs arose. Like Teotihuacan before it, it was a four-quartered city inspired by a cosmovision with several distinctive qualities.

Many cosmologies, or statements of world order, stress the achievement of stability, security, and control over the forces of chaos. The Aztec cosmology, however, had several distinctive qualities, including the fact that the cosmic setting was a dynamic, unstable, destructive one distinguished by sharp alternations between order and disorder, cosmic life, and cosmic death. This cosmic order was marked on both the celestial and terrestrial levels by combats, sacrifice, and rebellion as well as by harmony, cooperation, and stability. But the former actions always seemed to overcome the latter. The formal expression of this is the **Myth of the Suns,** which was carved in splendid symbolism on the face of the Calendar Stone, or Sun Stone, which stands today in the Museo Nacional de Antropología (National Museum of Anthropology) in Mexico City. The stone, along with a number of other pre-Columbian and postconquest accounts, depicts the Four Ages, or Four Suns, through which the universe passed prior to the present age, the Fifth Age.

The great Aztec Calendar Stone, carved sometime after 1502 CE during the reign of Moctezuma II. In the center is the sun god of the current age surrounded by four mythical dates that symbolize previous epochs of creation and destruction. The twenty-day signs circle the central core of the stone. Two sky serpents facing each other at the bottom represent time and space. (Photograph courtesy of Museo Nacional de Mexico.)

The First Age, called Sun 4-Tiger, was brought into order out of primordial chaos. Then a struggle between the gods ensued, resulting in a collapse of the cosmos and, according to one tradition, its reorganization by the winning deity, Tezcatlipoca. The beings who lived in this era were eaten by ocelots. This process of order and collapse was repeated four times. The Second Age was called Sun 4-Wind, and the beings who lived there were carried away by wind. The Third Age was Sun 4-Rain, and fire rained on people and they became turkeys. The Fourth Age was Sun 4-Water, and water swallowed the people and they became fish. Then, the present age, Sun-4 Movement, was created out of the sacrifice of a large number of deities in Teotihuacan, or elsewhere, depending on the tradition. It was believed that this age would end in earthquakes and famine. What is clear is that cosmic order is achieved in the Aztec universe out of conflict, sacrifice, and the death of humans and gods.

This cosmic understanding, that cosmic order comes from conflict and sacrifice, was at the basis of the extraordinary practices of bloodletting and human sacrifice throughout Mesoamerica. Each of the 18 twenty-day months involved the public sacrifices of captured warriors, or in rare cases children, or young women. But in each case the purpose was to acquire the divine forces embedded in the physiology of human beings in order to nourish the sun, earth, and rain so that the stability of the Fifth Age would be maintained. These ceremonies were elaborate musical, artistic, public displays of Aztec cosmology and political will.

Aztec ceremonies, guided by detailed ritual calendars, varied from settlement to settlement. Typically, however, they involved three stages: days of ritual preparation, ceremonial sacrifice, and acts of nourishing the gods and the community. The days of ritual preparation included fasting, lengthy processions (sometimes to many mountain and lake shrines), and offerings of food, flowers, and paper. There were extensive purification techniques, embowering, songs, and processions of deity impersonators (*teotl ixiptlas*) to different temples in ceremonial precincts. Following these elaborate preparations blood sacrifices were carried out on pyramidal and temple platforms by priestly groups trained to dispense the victims swiftly. This involved different types of **autosacrifice** (bleeding of self) and the heart sacrifice of enemy warriors and purchased slaves.

Though a variety of methods were used, including decapitation, burning, hurling from great heights, strangulation, and arrow sacrifice, the typical ritual involved the dramatic heart sacrifice and the placing of the heart in a ceremonial vessel (sometimes the *cuauhxicalli*-eagle vessel) in order to nourish the gods. We will look more deeply into the religious meaning of these amazing actions in the next chapter.

Aztec warfare was intimately tied to this cosmovision and ritual tradition. War, as we shall see, was a religious and aesthetic affair designed not only to dominate one's enemies but also to rejuvenate the deities by "debt-payment" (*nextlaoaliztli*), returning to the "Giver of Life" some of the sacred energy he had provided and sacrificed in the beginning and which needs rejuvenation each month. Reflecting themes we have seen as far back as Olmec times, war was the place "where the jaguars roar," where "feathered war bonnets heave about like foam in the waves." And death on the battlefield was called *xochimiquiztli,* the flowery death.

The entire situation of stability/instability, war, and empire is reflected in the **Xochiyaoyotl** or Wars of the Flowers, which were practiced between 1450 and 1519. These Flowery Wars consisted of a series of scheduled battlefield confrontations primarily between warriors from the Triple Alliance and warriors from the Tlaxcalan-Pueblan Valley Kingdoms to the east. The purpose of these wars, which pitted the most powerful eagle and jaguar knights of the Aztecs against their enemies, was to acquire sacrificial victims for the ritual festivals in the ceremonial centers, to keep warriors in training, and to reaffirm and raise the status of warriors. However, it is often overlooked that these Flowery Wars also had a vital political significance, namely to reestablish or disrupt the borders and balance of power between competing city-states.

All this activity was directed by *tlatoanis* or chief speakers, the name for lords or kings. The line of Aztec kings, which included the two Moctezumas (Ilhuicamina [1440–1454], and Moteuczoma Xocoyotzin [1503–1519], the king Westerners know as Montezuma), were warriors, priests, and artists all in one. But one of their primary responsibilities was to lead successful wars of conquest resulting in rich tributary payments of foods, luxuries, feathers, servants, and captured warriors in order to keep the capital rich and publicly triumphant, "the foundation of heaven."

But all was not conflict and aggression in Aztec religion. As we shall see in chapter 3 the Aztecs were skilled poets and philosophers who developed artistic techniques in order to realize human spiritual potential. These techniques included skillful linguistic formulations that were believed to enable the human personality to achieve elevated spiritual experiences and raise the human heart to unforeseen levels of insight and power. The practitioners of this ritual art, called the *tlamatinime* or "knowers of things," also developed, according to some scholars, a critique against the spiritual crisis caused by the dominant cosmovision of conflict and warfare. Rather than attempt to achieve knowledge of the divine through blood sacrifice, they argued that the Place of Duality or Omeyocan, referred to as the "innermost part of heaven," could be known through the creation of true words, or supreme poems, or aesthetic works. In this way the innermost self, the heart (*yollotl*), became inspired by a divine force—that is, was deified, and united with the gods in a spiritual sense rather than through heart sacrifice. One of the geniuses who developed this approach was the Tlatoani of Texcoco, **Nezahualcoyotl,** the Fasting Coyote. He was not only a poet, warrior, and spiritual leader of this ceremonial city, but also organized public festivals where Aztec arts and philosophy were presented and refined.

A number of other remarkable cultures and city-states shaped the course of Mesoamerican religions. Among important cultures we have not discussed were the Totonacs, Tarascans, Otomis, and Mixtecs. The latter culture in particular made a remarkable contribution through a series of beautifully painted pictorial histories depicting the Mixtec pantheon, ritual system of cosmogony, and cosmology. It is clear that the Mixtecs utilized a powerful calendric system to communicate sacred genealogies and the histories of royal families and towns. Several examples of this pictorial art appear in this book.

This historical overview has concentrated on a general chronology and creative moments in Mesoamerican ceremonial centers. Now we will take a look at the general cosmovision that has emerged. Although there were important variations in the different regions and periods of Mesoamerican history (and we have not covered many significant groups), it is fair to say that certain general patterns of worldmaking, worldcentering, and worldrenewing were shared by nearly all Mesoamerican cultures.

The Mesoamerican Cosmovision

As stated earlier, the term *cosmovision* points to the ways in which cultures combine their cosmological notions relating to time and space into a structural and systematic whole. The following discussion of the Mesoamerican cosmovision will be divided into the structure of the cosmos, the cosmic significance of the human being, and the patterns of time.

The Structure of the Cosmos

The Mesoamerican universe, in its various formulations, had a geometry consisting of three general levels: an overworld or celestial space; the middleworld or earthly level; and the underworld (Mictlan, Place of the Dead). One of the most sophisticated images of this universe appears on the sarcophagus lid of the ruler **Pacal** at Palenque, the majestic capital of the Classic Maya. We see all three levels of the cosmos expressed in the roots, trunk, branches, and top of the World Tree, which is embroidered with serpents, jewels, plants, mirrors, and other valuable items. There were, at least among the ancient Nahuas, thirteen celestial levels and nine underworld levels, each inhabited by diverse gods and supernatural beings, often depicted as conjugal pairs. The top level (in some sources there are nine celestial levels) was inhabited by Ometeotl, the God of Duality.

Each of these realms, which in the Nahua imagination were divided into smaller, powerful units, were permeated with supernatural powers circulating up and down the cosmic levels through spiral-shaped passages called *malinallis*. Some levels, especially the lower terrestrial and aquatic levels, including the mountains, were filled with abundant, valuable forces such as seeds, water, and precious stones upon which farmers, families, and craftsmen depended. One Mexican scholar notes that the ancient Nahuas

> believed this earthly and aquatic world to be contaminated by death and jealously guarded by the dangerous "lords" of springs and woods. Even today, the places from which wealth derives—fountains, forests and mines—are thought to be points of communication between the worlds of men and that of death, guarded by the Ohuican Chaneque, "lords of the dangerous places."[12]

In some versions of the universe these supernatural entities and forces flowed into the human level through giant ceiba trees, which held up the sky at the four quarters of the world and stood at the center of the universe. As we can see when we look at the ideal image of the universe as pictured in the *Codex Fejérváry Mayer,* the four-quartered universe is structured by four flowering trees, each with a supernatural bird on its crown. In some cultures a flowering tree or a sacred mountain stood at the center of the universe linking up, like a vertical shaft, the upper, middle, and lower worlds.

In Maya cosmology the souls of the dead and supernatural forces often traveled from level to level via the extravagant flowering trees at the axis of the universe. For instance the great Maya king Ah Pacal (Lord Shield) is pictured on his sarcophagus lid as falling down the shaft of this tree, along with the setting sun, into the gaping jaws of the earth monster after his death. But once in the underworld it was believed that he was transformed into a supernatural entity who continued to influence life on earth, especially at intersections between cosmic levels, such as the temples he built during his reign.

These supernatural forces, from below and above, could also enter the world through caves, fire, sunlight, animals, stones—any place where there was a spiral or opening connecting humans with the spaces or temporal cycles of the gods. In the Aztec cosmovision some of the pyramids or great temples in the ceremonial centers served as replicas of the cosmic mountain, or *axis mundi,* which in ritual performances connected the sun, stars, and celestial influences to earth. These monumental architectural structures were also seen as openings to the underworld and sometimes had caves or special rooms built at the base where subterranean forces could enter and exit the earthly level. The ceremonial centers of Teotihuacan, Palenque, Chichén Itzá, Tollan, and Tenochtitlan were organized as replicas of this cosmic geometry so that elites, warriors, captives, traders, farmers, poets, and commoners could experience this cosmovision and participate in its nurturance.

Cosmovision and the Human Being

Another type of "center" in Mesoamerican religions was the human being, especially the human body and the "career" of the human being. The three levels of the cosmos corresponded to the human body. *Ilhuicatl,* or heavenly water, was linked to the head, while one of the lower heavens was associated with the heart. The liver was linked to the spiritual forces of the underworld. As Alfred Lopez Austin has abundantly shown in *The Human Body and Ideology,* Mesoamerican peoples saw the human body as the nucleus and unifying body of the cosmos, which was permeated—in fact, "loaded"—with specific supernatural powers and entities. The human body was progressively filled—at conception, birth, the first exposure to fire and sunlight, and at points of special achievements in life—with powers originating in the celestial spaces above and in sacred events that took place in mythical time. Although all parts of the human body were loaded with these special powers, they were concentrated in three parts of the human physiology. The head (especially in the hair and in the fontanel area, the soft spot on an infant's skull) was filled with *tonalli,* an animating force or soul that provided vigor and the energy for growth and development. The heart received deposits of *teyolia* (what gives life to people), which provided emotion, memory, and knowledge to the human. This was the soul that could live and have influence after the body was dead. The liver received *ihiyotl,* which provided humans with bravery, desire, hatred, love, and happiness. It was thought of as a luminous gas that could attract and charm other people. These forces or "animating entities" directed the physiological process of a human body, gave the person character, and were highly valued by the family and sought after in warfare and ritual sacrifice. It was believed that some of these powers could be taken from a human body and either offered to the gods as a form of "debt payment" or acquired by the ritual person who touched the physical entity in which they resided.

Every human being was seen as the living center of these forces; but certain individuals—such as warriors, deity impersonators (*teotl ixiptla,* literally "images of the deity"), lords, or artists at the moment of creativity—contained extraordinary supernatural powers. One special type of human being, known to us through the reports of the Spanish chroniclers, was the *hombre-dios* or man-god who functioned as a religious virtuoso, an extraordinary model of religious conduct, power, and authority. These individuals were able to communicate directly, through the perception of their hearts, with the will and power of the deity, the symbols of whom they sometimes carried in sacred bundles. An outstanding example of this type of divine person was Topiltzin Quetzalcoatl, Our Lord the Plumed Serpent, the priest-king of Tollan. Tollan was the fabled and historical kingdom of the tenth-century Toltecs, who were renowned as having discovered the structure of the universe and having invented the most important worldrenewing rituals.

The Cosmovision of Time

One of the most fascinating aspects of Mesoamerican religions was the fact that time was believed to exist in three different planes, each intersecting with one another. The meeting of human time with the time of the gods and the time before the gods filled human life with incredible power, changes, and significance.

Human beings dwelled in a time or cycle of time created on the surface of the earth by the gods. It was marked by a yearly calendar. Time and space were seen as an intertwined sacred entity. The passage of time was created by supernatural forces that emanated from the sky and underworld and converged on the earthly level. In this manner human time and space was filled with sacred forces. There was another temporal cycle prior to human time in which the gods had undergone struggles, abductions, broken honor, death, and dismemberment. This cycle of time, the time of myths, had two special features influencing human experience within the first cycle of time. First, it resulted in the creation of supernatural beings who became intimately connected to daily life in human space on earth. Second, this cycle of time continues on into the present.

Beyond these two temporal realms, which touched each other constantly, was the third temporal realm, the transcendent time of the gods. The high gods existed prior to the other two cycles but provided the original energy and structure of the universe. This primordial time of the gods, when order first appeared out of chaos, continues on in a celestial realm. We can conceive of these cycles as a wheel within a larger wheel within a larger wheel. Each hour and day in the early time is in touch with the particular forces of the time of the gods and the time of myth. In this way human life (time and space) is loaded up with a specific set of powers and entities each day. And each day these powers and entities are different. Lopez Austin summarizes this multiple view of time in the following manner.

> The second time, the time of myth, did not end after it had given birth to the time of man. The time of myth continued ruling, far from man's dwelling place. . . . When a moment of human time coincided with one of the ever-present moments of mythical time, man's time received an imprint from the world of the gods. The sequence of correspondences between one and another time resulted in cycles of different dimensions, making each moment happening in human time a meeting place for a plurality of divine forces, all combining to constitute its particular nature. . . . Thus, an hour of the day was characterized by being a moment of night or day; by the influence of a sign (one among the twenty day names) and a number (one among thirteen) in a cycle of 260 days; by the group of thirteen to which it belonged; by its month (among eighteen) and its position within the month (among twenty) by the year (among fifty-two) which in its turn was marked by the destiny of a sign (among four) and a number (among thirteen); and so on, successively, through the sequence of other cycles. . . . This made each moment on earth a complex combination of the different influences coming down from the heavens or arising from the underworld.[13]

The Mesoamerican calendars (found in sculpture or in *tonala-matls,* books of day counts) marked and regulated the passage of influences into human life. One of the great measuring devices for these calendars was astronomical observations, which guided a number of major ceremonies related to Venus, the Pleiades, and changes in the solar cycle. In some cases entire ceremonial centers or parts of ceremonial centers were laid out so that dramatic observations of these astronomical events could be celebrated and communicated through public rituals. One such ceremony was the **New Fire Ceremony,** or Binding of the Years, which marked the passage of the Pleiades through the meridian at midnight once every fifty-two years or 18,980 nights. In fact the Pleiades passed through the zenith every night, but it only passed through the zenith at midnight once a year. The complexity of Aztec observation appears when we realize that they regarded only one of every fifty-two passages as supremely important because it marked the exhaustion of possible interactions between two different calendar systems. This ceremony included the ritual sacrifice of an enemy warrior to mark the rejuvenation of all cycles of time.

Within these complicated formulas of time was a profound commitment and concern for insuring the renewal of cosmic forces alive in plants, animals, humans, and dynasties. In Maya religion, for instance, bloodletting ceremonies by members of the royal household were enacted to bring the ancestors and deities and the time of myth into the realm of humans to nurture agriculture, empower a lord at the time of his enthronement, or prepare a community for war.

One dramatic ceremony, linking up the time of the gods with human time, involved the bloodletting ritual by **Lady Xoc** of Palenque. We see in the sculptures of Yaxchilán a giant, twisting, decorated serpent emerging from her blood. Out of the "jeweled serpent's" mouth comes what appears to be the body of a divine warrior returning to earth to empower the dynasty. It is through this ritual sacrifice that two realms of time, the time of the gods and the time of humans, are linked together and renewed.

Now that we have reconstructed parts of the history and structure of the ceremonial world and cosmovisions of Mesoamerica, it is time to examine the arresting case of Aztec religion, which was animated by the militancy of the warrior and the art of refined speech.

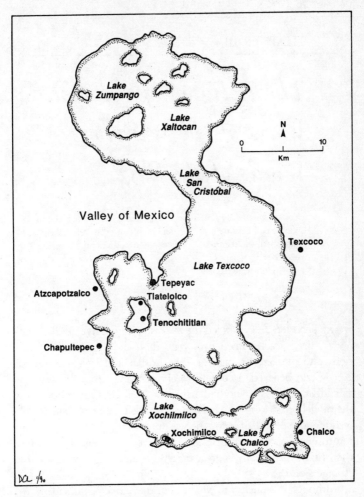

Map 2. Core Area of Aztec World

CHAPTER III

The Religion of the Aztecs: Ways of the Warrior, Words of the Sage

He was imitated by the incense keepers and the priests. The life of Quetzalcoatl became a pattern for the life of every priest: so it was established, the regimen of Tollan—so it was adopted here in Mexico.

Florentine Codex[1]

When Hernán Cortés led the Spanish army of five hundred soldiers, accompanied by several thousand allied Indian warriors, into the Aztec capital of Tenochtitlan in 1519, Moctezuma Xocoyotzin believed, according to one account, "that this was Topiltzin Quetzalcoatl who had arrived." Topiltzin Quetzalcoatl was the model priest-king who had ruled the great eleventh-century Toltec kingdom of Tollan before he was forced into exile, promising to return one day. Moctezuma sent a number of rich gifts, including the ritual costume of the great deity Quetzalcoatl, to welcome the strangers on the coast.

Although it is unclear to what extent the native peoples identified Cortés as the return of Quetzalcoatl or one of his descendants, it is clear that important elements of the Aztec cosmovision were based on the ancestral tradition of the Toltecs. As we saw in the previous chapter this tradition included an emphasis on the intimate relationship between the great god Quetzalcoatl and the *hombre-dios* Topiltzin Quetzalcoatl (Our Young Prince the Feathered Serpent). The Aztecs, as well as many other cultures, followed, in part, "the pattern" of Toltec religion when developing their cosmology, priest-

hood, and sacred architecture. The Aztec shape of time and ceremonial renewal, which provided the framework for ritual sacrifice including human sacrifice, was influenced by the Toltec tradition. The
identification of Cortés with the great priest-king of Tollan becomes
more plausible when we realize that, in Aztec belief, Topiltzin was
born in the year *ce acatl* (One Reed), departed his kingdom fifty-
two years later in *ce acatl,* and was expected to return in the year *ce
acatl.* It is one of the amazing coincidences of history that the Aztec
year *ce acatl* fell in the Christian year 1519, the year that Cortés
appeared in Mexico.[2]

The significant role that Topiltzin Quetzalcoatl played in Mesoamerican religions after the twelfth century points to a major pattern
in worldcentering. Each community was organized by expressions of
authority rooted in sacred traditions and events. Sacred authority
was often expressed in and through the career of certain exemplary
human lives or types of religious virtuosos. Many religions, especially religions organized by urban centers, develop elaborate conceptions of social and symbolic authority associated with high-status
positions and the paraphernalia associated with those positions. Religious authority can take many forms or be embedded in many
kinds of objects, such as the Crown of Charlemagne, the Chair of
the Pope, or the Chrysanthemum throne of the Japanese Emperor,
or in a sacred teaching like the Torah in Judaism. One of the most
widespread and influential forms of authority (that is, authority as
central value system and major symbols derived from tradition) is in
certain types of human beings such as prophets, founders, magi-
cians, seers, or saints. The lives and personal experiences of these
leaders embody the most sacred values and teachings of a tradition,
providing it with a central image or exemplary pattern for proper
conduct and religious devotion.

The Sacred Career of Topiltzin Quetzalcoatl

One of the most important ways in which a community expresses
these values and symbols of authority is through the telling of stories, hymns, legends, or gospels that grow up around the life and
death of a revered individual. In Mesoamerican capital cities from
the twelfth century on a rich tradition of stories, songs, paintings,

Quetzalcoatl Ehécatl as lord of the wind is seated upon a jaguar throne next to a giant feathered serpent. This image comes from the Codex Laud, *a preconquest deerskin screenfold manuscript. (Courtesy of Akademische Druck und Verlagsanstalt, Graz, Austria, 1966 facsimile ed.)*

and sculpture depicted to young and old alike the inspired career of Topiltzin Quetzalcoatl and his relationship with his powerful divinity.

This tradition told how divine forces, originating on other levels of the cosmos, entered the world through Topiltzin's life and religious experiences. This career can be compared to a seven-act play depicting his (1) miraculous birth, (2) ritual training and ecstatic experiences, (3) ascension to the throne, (4) creation of his splendid capital, (5) downfall at the hands of his rival, Tezcatlipoca, (6) exile, and (7) death and transformation into Venus as the Morning Star, a divinity. All these "acts" had influence in later history, but we will focus on his birth and ritual training for the priesthood; his career as a warrior/sacrificer; his splendid capital; and the manner of his death and transformation into the Morning Star. In this way we will come to see how parts of Aztec religion were patterned on the dramatic career of Topiltzin Quetzalcoatl.

Birth and Ritual Training

According to one tradition Topiltzin Quetzalcoatl was conceived after his mother Chimalma (Earth Shield) swallowed an emerald.

He was raised by his grandparents and underwent seven years of rigorous ritual training, living for a time as a mountain ascetic. He practiced autosacrifice, the bleeding of oneself through insertion of spines or other ritual implements into parts of one's body. These techniques were at once offerings to the gods and "openings" in the human body designed to enhance direct communication with deities. He also built ritual temples in order to meditate, pray, chant, and carry out sacrifices. His influence on Aztec ceremonial life was discovered by the sixteenth-century Spanish friar, Diego Durán, who interviewed Aztec survivors of the wars with the Spanish. Durán wrote,

> all the ceremonies and rites, building temples and altars and placing idols in them, fasting, going nude and sleeping . . . on the floor, climbing mountains to preach the law there, kissing the earth, eating it with one's fingers and blowing trumpets and conch shells and flutes on the great feast days—all these things imitated the ways of the holy man, Topiltzin Quetzalcoatl.[3]

One of the most valued achievements in this holy man's career was his direct experience of Ometeotl, the Creative Heavenly Pair who dwelt in the innermost part of heaven at the top of the celestial levels. One text tells that in the year Two Reed, Ce Acatl Quetzalcoatl (another name for the hero) built a special temple facing the cardinal directions and fasted, did penance, and bathed in icy cold waters. He also set thorns into his flesh on the summit of four sacred mountains near Tollan. Following these ritual ordeals, he

> sent up his prayers, his supplications into the heart of the sky and called out to Skirt of Stars, Light of Day, Lady of Sustenance, Wrapped in Coal, Wrapped in Black, She who endows the earth with solidity, He who covers the earth with cotton.

This quest to communicate with the High God is successful, for

> they knew that he was crying out to the place of Duality, which lies above the ninefold heaven. And thus they knew, they who dwell there, that he called upon them and petitioned them most humbly and contritely.[4]

These techniques of humble prayers, autosacrifice, bathing in cold water, and speaking in metaphors of duality became the priestly style for opening paths of communication with celestial forces in the Toltec world and in subsequent city-states, including the Aztec capital.

Model Warrior/Sacrificer

A controversial part of Topiltzin Quetzalcoatl's career was his experience as a warrior. During his lifetime he apparently changed his attitude toward war and ritual sacrifice, which were intimately linked throughout Mesoamerican history.

Topiltzin Quetzalcoatl was born into a world of war. According to many primary sources the gods were periodically at war with one another during the mythic eras prior to human existence. In the vivid creation story of the *Historia de los Mexicanos por Sus Pinturas,* the gods created the Chichimec people in order to gain sacrificial blood through human warfare and the ritual sacrifice of captive warriors. Within this cosmic order Topiltzin Quetzalcoatl spent seven years of ritual training to become a warrior, utilizing sacred forces to enhance his battlefield experience. He fights gallantly alongside his father, who is killed and buried in the sand by enemies. Topiltzin recovers his father's body and buries him at a shrine on Cloud Serpent Mountain. Enemy warriors led by Apanetcatl attack him, and Topiltzin

> rose up, striking him full in the face, sent him tumbling down, and he fell to the base of the mountain. Next he seized Zolton and Cuilton and . . . he put them to death, he spread them with chili and slashed their flesh and he set out to make conquests.[5]

This action of attacking enemies and performing human sacrifices at mountain shrines became a model for Aztec warfare and sacrificial ceremonies, as we shall see in the upcoming section on the Great Aztec Temple.

However, according to several traditions, Topiltzin Quetzalcoatl initiated a reformation in sacrificial practices later in his career: He forbade human sacrifice. One text reads,

> And it is told and related that many times during the life of Quetzalcoatl certain sorcerers attempted to shame him into making human offerings, into sacrificing humans. But he would not consent. He would not comply, because he loved his subjects who were Tol-

tecs. The offerings he made were only of snakes, birds, and butterflies.[6]

This reformation provoked the trickery of a rival cult led by the priest of Tezcatlipoca, Lord of the Smoking Mirror. Topiltzin, now the wise king of Tollan, was tricked into a drunken episode during which he violated his priestly vows and was forced to abdicate and flee into exile.

One text describes his lament at his downfall:

Thereupon Quetzalcoatl said, "Unfortunate me!" Then he raised his lament he'd composed for his going away. And he sang:

"No more.
The days will be counted no more in my house and it
    shall be empty."

Then his pages weeping sing,

"No more we delight in him,
Him our noble one,
Him Quetzalcoatl
No more thy precious crown!"[7]

This tension between sacrificing human beings or using other means to open ways of communicating with the deities continued on into Aztec history, as we shall see in the upcoming section on sacred words. For now let us look briefly at what the Aztecs claimed Topiltzin Quetzalcoatl lost as a result of this great defeat.

The Splendid City

When the Aztec elders spoke to Bernardino de Sahagun after the conquest about the cultural sources of their achievements, they stated that it was the Toltecs "who came to cause the cities to be founded." The Toltecs were considered the ancient geniuses who set culture on a new level of excellence. "The Tolteca were wise. Their works were all good, all perfect, all wonderful, all miraculous; their houses beautiful, tiled in mosaics, smoothed, stuccoed, very marvelous."[8] In fact the elders were describing the splendid city of Tollan, which emerged during the reign of Topiltzin Quetzalcoatl. It was remembered as having been the greatest urban achievement in human history. This grand prestige was due to the environmental and artistic plenitude of Quetzalcoatl's kingdom.

The wealth of Toltec fields was like an ancient Findhorn: All the "squashes were very large, and some quite round. And the ears of maize were as large as hand grinding stones, and long. They could hardly be embraced in one's arms." And the amaranth plants, so important in Aztec agriculture and ritual offerings, were as tall as trees, "verily they climbed up them; they could be climbed." Also the cotton farming produced fields of amazing colors, "burnt red, yellow, rose colored, violet, green, azure, verdigris color, whitish, brown, shadowy, rose red and coyote colored . . . so they grew; they did not dye them."[9]

This part of the ecological complex was matched in excellence by the technological and artistic achievements of the Toltecs. The people of Quetzalcoatl were remembered as the finest feather workers, physicians, jewelers, astronomers, architects. Their ritual buildings were constructed to face the cardinal directions: The eastern building was the house of gold, the western building was the house of fine turquoise, the southern building was the house of shells and silver, and the northern house was inlaid with red precious stones. The achievements of these people are summed up in this passage: "In truth they invented all the wonderful, precious, marvelous things which they made . . . "

But this splendid urban achievement of cosmovision, agricultural abundance, and technological excellence began to crumble when the priest-king went into exile.

Death and Deification of the Human Body

The exile of Topiltzin Quetzalcoatl was a well-known story in the Aztec capital. The places he stopped to rest, eat, and search for ritual objects are mentioned in the narratives about the fall of his kingdom. In one place it is known, from indentations on rocks, that he put his buttocks there. The religious meaning of his life becomes clear when he arrives at the seacoast (referred to as the celestial shore of divine water), weeps, and discards his ornaments, green mask, and feathers. Realizing that his earthly career has run its course, he sacrifices himself by cremation, and

> from his ashes, rose all the precious birds, the cotinga, the spoonbill, the parrots . . . Then the heart of Quetzalcoatl rose into heaven and,

according to the elders, was transformed into the Morning Star . . . and Quetzalcoatl was called Lord of the Dawn.[10]

This episode points to one of the most pervasive notions in Aztec religion: the sacrality of the human body and its potential to return its energy to the celestial forces that created it. It was widely believed that at death energies within the human body, especially the *teyolia* contained in the human heart, could become deified or grafted onto the celestial substance of a divinity. In this case Topiltzin Quetzalcoatl's *teyolia* becomes the planet Venus in its appearances as the morning star.

As we now turn to discussions of Aztec cosmology, temples, speech arts, and sacrifice, we will see why the Aztecs chanted, "From him it began, from Quetzalcoatl it flowed out, all art and knowledge."

Cosmovision and the Human Body

A prayer to Tezcatlipoca, spoken in the Aztec capital, and recorded by Sahagun:

> O master, O our lord, O lord of the near, of the nigh, O night, O wind: thou seest, thou knowest things within the trees, the rocks. And behold now, it is true that thou knowest of things within us: thou hearest us from within. Thous hearest, thou knowest that which is withn us: what we say, what we think; our minds, our hearts.[11]

The history of religions teaches us that, at one time or another, almost everything has been considered sacred. Archaeological, textual, and ritual evidence shows that during the long and diverse experiences of the human species gestures, toys, games, books, buildings, animals, stars, sex, hunting, food, even athletics have been considered religious in nature. More specifically we see that there are holy books (Torah, Vedas, Sutras, Gospels, I Ching, Koran), sacred buildings, (St. Peter's, the Ka'ba, the Basilica of Guadalupe); sacred cities (Ife, Kyoto, Jerusalem, Rome); sacred mountains (Mt. Fuji, Mt. Sinai, Mt. Tlaloc); sacred people (Jesus, the Buddha, Joseph Smith, Confucius, Topiltzin Quetzalcoatl); and sacred offices (papacy, ayatollah, *ashiwanni*—Zuni rain priests). We also have persuasive evidence that in a number of cultures the human body is understood as a sacred container of cosmic powers.

The central ritual in Christianity, for example, is the ingestion of the "body and blood" of Jesus. His body, filled with divine love, is symbolically or actually (according to the particular tradition) taken into other human bodies, which become spiritually renewed. In the Buddhist tradition the bodily remains of Sakyamuni Buddha were believed to have been deposited in stupas or stone monuments after the Buddha's death. As time passed these stupas became objects of pilgrimage. Eventually new stupas were built to house the bodily remains and relics associated with outstanding Buddhist sages. In some cases pious Buddhists built their homes nearby so as to live close to these bodily remains. In a number of American Indian traditions vision quests included the offering of parts of bodies including skin, muscle, and fingers.

One of the most amazing examples of the sacred nature of the human body is the cult of mummies developed in Egypt and South America. In Egypt a chemical method was used to preserve the anointed and bandaged dead body so that the soul, which left at death, could return to take the food offerings left behind. Among the Inca of the fifteenth and sixteenth centuries in Peru, the bodies of rulers were mummified and consulted on major matters of state by living rulers, who believed that the deified, royal personality resided in the corpse. These mummies were housed in special temples and cared for by a group of specialists.

These diverse examples point to the importance of the human body in religious traditions. One of the most elaborate ritual expressions of the human body as a container of sacred forces was developed in Mesoamerica. In this section we will survey how Aztec peoples saw the human organism as the container *par excellence* of sacred powers and rhythms. On certain ritual occasions the human physique was treated as an extremely potent living image of cosmic forces. This study will prepare us for our discussion of the most difficult topics facing students of Mesoamerica: bloodletting and human sacrifice.

The Body at the Center of the World

We have seen that Mesoamerican religions were most vividly expressed in ceremonial centers. The most pervasive type of sacred space where elaborate ceremonies were carried out was the human body. The human body was considered a potent receptacle of cosmological forces, a living, moving center of the world.

Consider, for instance, the elaborate image of the cosmos from the *Codex Fejérváry Mayer*. It reflects the typical Mesoamerican worldview divided into five sections. We see the four quarters, each containing a sacred tree with a celestial bird on top, surrounding the central region where **Xiuhtecuhtli,** the Fire God, is dressed in warrior regalia. According to scholars the body of Tezcatlipoca has been cut into pieces and divided over the four directions of the world, with his blood flowing into the center. The divine blood is flowing into the axis of the universe, which redistributes the divine energy to animals, body parts, vegetation, and the calendar, which is divided by the four quarters of the cosmos. Each quadrant shows two of the Nine Lords of the Night in ritual postures next to the cosmic tree. The dots surrounding the edges of the design represent the 260-day ritual calendar divided by the spatial structure of the universe.

In order to understand the religious power of the human body and to build a foundation for our discussion of human sacrifice, let us focus on the importance of two body parts in Aztec religions, the heart and the head.

The Mesoamerican cosmos was conceived as a series of thirteen celestial and nine underworld layers, each layer inhabited by gods, supernatural beings, and forces. These powers and beings entered the earthly level through a series of openings or avenues of communication including the four cosmic trees at the edges of the world, mountains, caves, the rays of the sun, the motion of the wind, and so forth. These lines of communication were pictured as two pairs of heliacal bands, called *malinalli,* which moved in constant motion, allowing the forces of the underworld to ascend and the forces of the overworld to descend. In this way the Turquoise World (sky) and the Obsidian World (underworld) were dynamically connected to the terrestrial world of nature, human beings, and society. These supernatural forces emerged each day from the sacred trees and spread across the landscape. They could be introduced into the human body by either ritual means or through the action of nature.

Page 1 of the Codex Frejérváry-Mayer *is a schematic representation of the cosmos, depicting the center and the four cardinal directions. It is also a divinatory calendar used to predict the fortune of future events. The Mesoamerican concepts of time and space were intimately linked to geographical and cosmological relationships. (Courtesy of Akademische Druck und Verlagsanstalt, Graz, Austria, 1971 facsimile ed.)*

Tonalli

One of the most powerful divine forces was called *tonalli* (from *tona,* to irradiate or make warm with sun), which was collected in the human head. The original source of *tonalli* was Ometeotl, the supreme Dual God residing at the top of the thirteen celestial layers. But the divine *tonalli* reached the human through the action of celestial beings inhabiting other levels of the sky. It was believed that at the moment of the conception of a human being Ometeotl intervened on one of the celestial levels and sent vital energy into the uterus of the female. This energy was deposited into the head of the embryo, resulting in the original shape of one's temperament and destiny. After the child was born containing this initial amount of *tonalli,* the child was ritually placed near a fire and eventually exposed to the sun in order to increase his or her *tonalli*. Although the sun was believed to be the most powerful visible source of *tonalli*, people could acquire *tonalli* from beings close to them after birth.

The term *tonalli* has a rich range of meanings referring to its vigor, warmth, solar heat, summertime, and soul. It infiltrated animals, gods, plants, humans, and objects used in rituals. The hair that covered the head, especially the fontanel area, was a major receptacle of *tonalli*. The hair prevented the *tonalli* from leaving the body and was therefore a major prize in warfare. It was believed that the fortitude and valor of a warrior resided, in part, in the hair, and we have many pictorial scenes showing Aztec warriors grabbing the hair of enemies. The hair of warriors captured in battle was kept by the captors in order to increase their *tonalli*. The decapitated head of enemy warriors were a supreme prize for the city, which gained more *tonalli* through the ceremony.

Teyolia

Another divine force animating the human body was *teyolia*, which resided in the human heart. *Teyolia* was likened to "divine fire," and it animated the human being and gave shape to a person's sensibilities and thinking patterns. Every human heart contained this divine fire, but an extraordinary amount resided in the hearts of priests, *hombre-dioses*, artists, and the men and women who impersonated deities during festivals. Each of these human types was considered a living channel of *teyolia* into the social world. Extraordinary ritual achievements resulted in the increase of one's *teyolia*.

When a person died his or her *teyolia* traveled to the world of the dead, known as the "sky of the sun," where it was transformed into birds. This is the pattern of spiritual transformation we saw in the cremation of Topiltzin Quetzalcoatl. It was his *teyolia* that rose to heaven and changed into a divinity. This is the power to give energy to the sun, which was sought in the heart sacrifice of warriors. As one text says clearly, "Therefore, the ancients said that when they died, men did not perish, but began to live again almost as if awakened from a dream and that they became spirits or gods."[12]

Teyolia resided in mountains, lakes, towns, and temples. All important landscapes and living entities had *teyolia* or "heart." Each community had an *altepeyollotl* or heart of the town, a living divine force sometimes represented in a sculpture or decorated image. During the recent excavation of the Great Aztec Temple a number of statues were discovered representing the *teyolia* or heart of the sacred mountain. Our discussion now turns to a description and interpretation of this most powerful of Aztec places.

Serpent Mountain: The Great Aztec Temple

The Mesoamerican cosmos was centered in the physical characteristics of the human body. In this way each human being was a center of vital forces and changes. But each community had a public ceremonial precinct, which oriented all human activity and influenced social life. The most powerful sacred place in the Aztec empire was Coatepec or Serpent Mountain, the ritual name of the Great Temple of Tenochtitlan.

This identification of the great shrine with a sacred mountain points to one of the major religious patterns in Mesoamerican traditions, namely the identification of mountains as prodigious resources for abundance, danger, sacrality, and power. The Aztec temple/symbolic mountain stood in the center of the ceremonial precinct of the capital, which was the political center of an empire of more than four hundred towns and fifteen million people. The **Templo Mayor** of Tenochtitlan was significant not only because it supported the shrines of the great gods Tlaloc (god of rain and agriculture) and Huitzilopochtli (god of tribute and war), but also because, as the recent excavation of the structure revealed, it contained more than a hundred rich caches of ritual offerings buried in its floors.

Our discussion of the Great Temple will cover three important dimensions of Aztec religion: the theme of sacred mountains, the Aztec foundation myth, and the birth of the War God, Huitzilopochtli.

Cosmovision and the Sacred Mountain

One of the last impressions the Spaniards had of the Great Temple before the siege and conquest of the capital of Tenochtitlan in-

volved a desperate sacrifice of a number of their fellow soldiers by
the Aztecs. The Spanish soldier Bernal Díaz del Castillo describes
the Spanish retreat from a ferocious battle near the Great Temple.
Looking back toward the center of the city they saw the following:

> there was sounded the dismal drum of Huichilobos and many other
> shells and horns and things like trumpets and the sound of them all
> was terrifying, and we all looked toward the lofty Pyramid where
> they were being sounded, and saw that our comrades whom they
> had captured when they defeated Cortés were being carried by force
> up the steps, and they were taking them to be sacrificed. When they
> got them up to a small square in front of the oratory, where their
> accursed idols are kept, we saw them place plumes on the heads of
> many of them and with things like fans in their hands they forced
> them to dance before Huichilobos and after they had danced they
> immediately placed them on their backs on some rather narrow
> stones which had been prepared as places for sacrifice, and with
> some knives they sawed open their chests and drew out their palpi-
> tating hearts and offered them to the idols that were there, and they
> kicked the bodies down the steps, and the Indian butchers who were
> waiting below cut off the arms and feet and flayed the skin off their
> faces, and prepared it afterwards like glove leather with the beards
> on, and kept those for the festivals when they celebrated drunken
> orgies and the flesh they ate in chilimole.[13]

This amazing, shocking scene can only begin to make sense to us if
we attempt to understand a few of the major assumptions associated with Aztec cosmovision.

The Aztecs called their world *cemanahuac*, or "land surrounded by water." This land was conceived as having five parts with
four quadrants called *nauchampa*, literally the four directions of the
wind, extending outward from the central section. Each of these
quadrants were associated with specific names, colors, and influences. Though the pattern varied from culture to culture a typical
Mesoamerican version was: East—Tlacopan, Place of Dawn, yellow, fertile, and good; North—Mictlampa, Region of the Underworld, red, barren, and bad; West—Cihuatlampa, Region of
Women, blue, green, unfavorable, humid; South—Huitzlampa,
Region of Thorns, white; Center—Tlalxico, Navel, black. The waters surrounding the inhabited land were called *ilhuica-atl*, the celestial water, which extended upward in a vertical direction
merging with the sky and supporting the lower levels of heaven.

A reconstructed model of the Aztec ceremonial center in Tenochtitlan. The twin pyramid complex in the background was dedicated to two principal deities in Aztec cosmology, Tlaloc, representing water and fertility, and Huitzilopochtli, representing war and tribute. The circular temple in the foreground was dedicated to Quetzalcoatl Ehecatl, as lord of the wind. (Photograph courtesy of Lawrence G. Desmond.)

Through the navel flowed the vertical cosmos, which consisted of thirteen layers above and nine layers below the earth. As we saw in our historical overview of the Aztec city, it was believed to be the quintessential connecting point of the Above and the Below.

In Aztec cosmovision there were many connecting points between the supernatural spheres and the human sphere. The most outstanding examples were mountains, considered to be the sources of life-giving waters, deities, and diseases associated with rain, the *tlalocs* (rain gods), and other supernatural powers. The crucial role played by mountains in Aztec religion is reflected in the Nahuatl term for village, city, or community, **altepetl**, meaning "mountain filled with water." The human community with its various ceremonial centers was defined in terms of the landscape, the Mountain of Sustenance, which provided the resources for life. The many mountains surrounding the valley of Mexico were conceived as huge hollow vessels or "houses" filled with water that came from subterranean streams that filled the space beneath the earth. This underworld realm was called Tlalocan, considered the paradise of the great water deity Tlaloc. In this way the mountains were also *axis mundis* linking the watery underworld with the terrestrial level of the city to the celestial realms.

With this symbolism in mind we can turn back to the Great Aztec Temple with fresh understanding. The Great Temple consisted of a huge pyramidal base that supported two major shrines. Two stairways led up to the shrines of Tlaloc and Huitzilopochtli. The south side of the pyramid represented the legendary Coatepetl, the mountain birthplace of the war god Huitzilopochtli. The north side of the temple represents the Mountain of Sustenance associated with Tlaloc's paradise, which provided the precious rains and moisture that regenerated the agricultural world of the capital. Imagine the visual power this pyramid/temple had on the populace, who saw it standing in the center of the city as a living image of these two great mythic mountains.

A Myth of Foundation

This "symbolism of the center" is expressed in two important myths or sacred stories about Tenochtitlan. Both stories focus on the worldcentering character of the Templo Mayor and the surrounding sacred precinct.

How Tenochtitlan became the center of the world is told in the Aztec foundation myth, a version of which is embroidered on the flag of modern Mexico. Fortunately we have an excellent depiction of this act of worldcentering from the frontispiece of the *Codex Mendoza,* a valuable pictorial manuscript painted by native artists a decade after the conquest. The first image of the codex pictures a huge eagle, *nopal,* and stone above a giant Aztec shield with seven eagle-down feathers and seven arrows attached to it. The eagle represents the god Huitzilopochtli landing on the spot where the Aztecs were to build their major temple, around which the entire community developed. According to Aztec lore Huitzilopochtli had earlier appeared to the tribe's *hombre-dios,* ordering him to lead the people south until they say the image of the god sitting on the cactus. The shield with feathers and arrows is the ideogram for "place of authority" and the painted image can be read, "The Aztecs have arrived in Tenochtitlan, the place of authority." The long-range truth of this image—capital equals center of world

The Coyolxauhqui Stone, a large sculptured disc, 11 feet in diameter, depicting the dismembered Aztec goddess, Coyolxauhqui, who according to myth was dismembered by Huitzilopochtli, the patron deity of warfare and tribute among the Aztecs. (Photograph, David Hiser.)

equals place of authority—is demonstrated by the fact that when Cortés wrote his second letter to the King of Spain in 1520 he reported that "all the Lords of the land who are vassals of the said Montezuma have houses in the city and reside therein for a certain time of year." In other words all the leaders in the empire were lodged in the capital, lending it extra prestige as the place of authority.

As this discussion shows the central force in the foundation of the city, in the making of this social and architectural world, was the Aztec god Huitzilopochtli. He inspired the ancestors of the Aztecs to take the risky journey to find their distant home. He was also renowned for setting "men's hearts on fire and preparing them for war." In fact Aztec mythology is permeated with warrior themes and symbolism. Nowhere is this military aspect of their culture more evident than in the *teocuitatl* or divine song, a kind of epic poem about Huitzilopochtli's birth at Coatepec, the Serpent Mountain.

The divine song of Huitzilopochtli's birth goes like this. On Coatepec (Serpent Mountain) the mother of the gods, Coatlicue

(Lady of the Serpent Skirt) was sweeping out the temple. A ball of plumage "descended upon her" and she placed it in her bosom. Later she discovered it had disappeared and immediately realized she was pregnant. When the *centzon huitznahua* (the four hundred southerners, her children) heard of this pregnancy started at the sacred shrine, they were outraged. The text tells of this outrage:

> they were very angry, they were very agitated, as if the heart had gone out of them. Coyolxauhqui incited them, she inflamed the anger of her brothers, so that they should kill their mother.[14]

Led by the warrior sister **Coyolxauhqui,** the four hundred southerners

> felt very strong, adorned, decorated for war, they distributed among themselves their vestments of paper, their destiny, their nettles. . . . their arrows had sharp points . . . they went in order, in an orderly squadron, Coyolxauhqui guided them.

Coatlicue was frightened for her life, but a voice spoke to her from her womb: "Have no fear, already I know what I must do." The army in full fury rushed the mountaintop. Just at the moment of attack the god Huitzilopochtli sprang from his mother's womb full grown, dressed as a warrior, and engaged his brothers and sisters in combat. He grabbed a serpent of fire, charged his sister in a rage, and decapitated her in one swipe. The text reads, "her body went falling below and it went crashing to pieces in various places, her arms, her legs, her body kept falling."

As is the case with all mythology there are several layers of meaning to this influential story. At one level Huitzilopochtli's birth and victorious battle against the four hundred siblings represents the solar dimension of Aztec religion. It represents the daily sunrise above the sacred mountain (earth) and the elimination of the moon (Coyolxauhqui) and the stars (*centzon huitzhanua*). Second, this daily experience of nature is viewed in terms of a celestial conflict, war, and sacrifice. The natural order is a violent order. The world is renewed through ritual combat at the sacred mountain.

A third level of significance in the myth is historical. Records tell of a crucial battle at a mountain called Coatepec in which a leader named Huitzilopochtli killed an enemy woman warrior named Coyolxauhqui and decapitated her.

It is important to focus on the meaning of Coatepec in the drama. The Templo Mayor, called Coatepec by the Aztecs, consisted of a huge pyramid base supporting two temples, one to Huitzilopochtli and one to Tlaloc. Two grand stairways led up to the shrines. The Coyolxauhqui stone was found in 1978, during the excavation of the remains of the Great Temple, directly at the base of the stairway leading up to Huitzilopochtli's temple. On both sides of the stone and the two stairway were two large, grinning serpent heads. The Templo Mayor is the image of Coatepec or Serpent Mountain. Just as Huitzilopochtli triumphed at the top of the mountain, while his sister was dismembered and fell to pieces below, so Huitzilopochtli's temple and icon sat triumphantly at the top of Templo Mayor while the carving of the dismembered goddess was placed at the base of the stairway far below.

Most interpretations of the myth end with the dismemberment of Coyolxauhqui and the realization that the Templo Mayor and the architectural arrangement of Huitzilopochtli's temple and the Coyolxauhqui stone represent the drama of the myth. However, if we read on, we discover the mythic source for large-scale human sacrifice.

Following the dismemberment of Coyolxauhqui, Huitzilopochtli turns and attacks the rest of his siblings, "the four hundred gods of the south, he drove them away, he humbled them."

This increment of sacrifice is made emphatic in the text. After driving the four hundred off the mountain of the snake, Huitzilopochtli

> pursued them, he chased them like rabbits, all around the mountain
> . . . with nothing could they defend themselves. Huitzilopochtli
> chased them, he drove them away, he humbled them, he destroyed
> them, he annihilated them.

This mythic action of sacrifice on the sacred mountain, an elaboration of the sacrificial pattern in the early part of Topiltzin Quetzalcoatl's career, became a model in Aztec times for the sacrifice of large numbers of enemy warriors at the Great Temple of Tenochtitlan. Now we can see the meaning of that sacrifice of Spanish soldiers, which opened this section of our study. Much more than just a butchering of Spaniards was taking place. For when they ascended the Great Temple, dressed in plumes, and

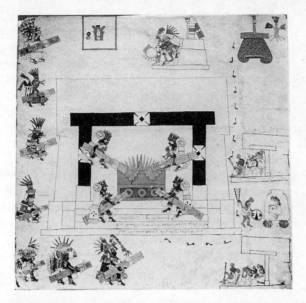

The New Fire Ceremony was performed at midnight every fifty-two years at the beginning/end of each calendar round. Seven deity impersonators with a fire-making implement are about to produce the fire of the new age that will be relayed to extinguished hearths throughout the empire. From the Aztec manuscript, Codex Borbonicus, *page 34. (Courtesy of Akademische Druck und Verlagsanstalt, Graz, Austria, 1974 facsimile ed.)*

danced before Huitzilopochtli's image, they were being forced to reenact the myth of the attack of the Four Hundred Southerners at Serpent Mountain. And as in the myth they were sacrificed, dismembered, and thrown down the sacred steps in order to give power to the Aztec age of the Fifth Sun.

Sacred Words

Among the Mexicans, . . . the wise, superior, and effective rhetoricians were held in high regard. And they elected these to be high priests, lords, leaders, and captains, no matter how humble their estate. These ruled the states, led the armies, and presided in the temples.[15]

It is erroneous to think of Aztec society and religion as primarily concerned with violence and aggression. As the pictorial images and ethnographic texts show, Nahuatl-speaking peoples worked cooperatively in farming communities, developed exquisite crafts and art forms, sponsored poetry festivals, cared deeply for children, worried about the power of gossip, loved telling stories, and warmed to the excitement, color, and tensions of the marketplace. All of these activities, the human life cycle, cultural expressions, farming, and trading were regulated and renewed by ceremonial performances.

Like all traditional urban societies the Aztec world was permeated by a formal sense of order and beauty. Feather work, dance, pottery, sculpture, mural painting, and philosophical discourse were vivid elements of the social landscape. One of the most refined and influential art forms was human speech. The Aztecs and their neighbors put great effort into developing both eloquent speech forms and profound metaphorical content in their spoken interactions. It is not easy for contemporary students, raised in a culture where "free speech" is a leading guide to language usage, to appreciate the power and meaning of those languages based on traditionally formal speech patterns and expressions. But Nahuatl was a highly formalized language that has often led outsiders to misunderstand its intentions and meanings. When Moctezuma Xocoyotzin greeted Hernan Cortés, for instance, he used conventional Nahuatl polite speech, which elevated the Spanish leader to a level of high honor. A number of scholars unfamiliar with Aztec language arts wrongly concluded that the welcoming speech showed the ruler to be a weak and docile leader. In fact he was greeting a state visitor in the proper respectful style of a welcoming Tlatoani.

When the Franciscan priest Bernardino de Sahagun did his extraordinary study of Aztec life and language in the 1540s, he discovered how florid, elegant, and meaningful Indian languages were. The most beautiful single volume of the twelve-volume encyclopedic *Florentine Codex* is Book VI, *Rhetoric and Moral Philosophy,* which presents the formal speeches and moral philosophy of the Aztecs. It contains forty extensive prayers, some over five pages long, plus exhortations and orations spoken by parents, rulers, midwives, and citizens. This remarkable volume concludes with a collection of proverbs, riddles, and metaphors portraying wit, insight, and vivid imagery.

These verbal arts, filled with beauty and complexity of thought, are comparable to the great literatures of the world. We will discuss three dimensions: the *tlamatinime*, or wise people trained in verbal arts; the *huehuetlatolli*, or the Ancient Word; and riddles. In each case we will see how the cosmovision of Mesoamerica turned speech into a ceremony between humans.

The Tlamatinime

Although rhetorical polish was appreciated in many social situations, there was a group of trained specialists, *tlamatinime* (knowers of things) who used the art of language to raise philosophical questions about human nature and its relations to ultimate truth. This group explored an alternate religious worldview to the mystico-military religion of the Aztec warrior class. They used language, instead of blood, to communicate and make offerings to the gods.

Compared to "a stout torch that does not smoke," the *tlamatinime* were trained in *calmecacs*, or schools of higher learning, to be ideal guides in human affairs. They preserved honored traditions, produced and read the painted manuscripts, and developed refined metaphors and poems to probe the true foundations of human existence. The clearest examples of its expression come from a series of texts showing the talents and insights of such rulers as Nezahualcoyotl (Fasting Coyote), King of Texcoco, Tecayehuatzin, Prince of Huexotzinco, and a dozen other *tlamatinime*. In other words this type of verbal art was largely practiced by the elites.

These poet-philosophers saw human existence as essentially fragile and ephemeral, as this poem attributed to Nezahualcoyotl indicates.

> I comprehend the secret, the hidden:
> O my lords!
> Thus we are,
> we are mortal,
> men through and through,
> we all will have to go away,
> we all will have to die on earth.
> Like a painting,
> we will be erased.

> Like a flower,
> we will dry up
> here on earth . . .
> Think on this my lords,
> eagles and ocelots,
> though you be of jade,
> though you be of gold
> you also will go there
> to the place of the fleshless.[16]

The precious aspects of life (jade, gold, flowers, paintings) are transitory and vulnerable rather than solid and with a firm foundation. Faced with this cosmic condition of instability and illusion, the *tlamatinime* developed a rhetorical strategy aimed at discovering and experiencing the nature of truth, a solid foundation to existence. They believed that there was such a reality beyond human existence, "in the region of the gods above and in the region of the dead below." in order to penetrate these regions and discover a stable reality, they had to devise techniques to open the depths of the human personality to the illusive world of truth. The main technique was the creation of **in xochitl, in cuicatl,** or flowers and songs, artistic expressions in the forms of words, songs, and paintings that connected the human personality, referred to as "face and heart," with the divine.

The Fasting Coyote also wrote of this connection,

> My flowers will not come to an end,
> my songs will not come to an end,
> I, the singer, raise them up:
> they are scattered, they are bestowed.[17]

Speaking of the power of poetry to express a lasting truth, he wrote,

> Even though flowers on earth
> may wither and yellow,
> they will be carried there,
> to the interior of the house
> of the bird with the golden feathers.[18]

This approach of linking the "face and heart" (personality) to the divine through the medium of "flower and song" was based on a religious conception of duality. In Nahuatl culture the cosmos was originally created and structured by a supreme Dual God, Ometeotl. This duality was manifested in the dualities, which combined to make forms of reality such as male/female, hot/cold, left/right, underworld/celestial world, above/below, darkness/light, rain/drought, death/life. At the level of human language this duality could be expressed in metaphors that generally consisted of two words or phrases joined to form a single idea, like "flower and song," meaning poetry or truth. At the level of the gods the High God or Ometeotl (Giver of Life) was the combined forces of Ometecuhtli and Omecihuatl. The language form used to inculcate this divine duality into words, called a *difrasismo,* includes two phrases joined to mean one thing. For example:

> *in xochitl, in cuicatl* = flower and song, = poetry or truth
> *in atl, in tepetl* = water and hill = a town
> *in topan, in mictlan* = what is above us, the region of the dead = the world beyond humans
> *topco, petlacalco* = in the bag and in the box = a secret
> *in cueitl, in huipilli* = the skirt, the blouse = the sexual nature of women.

In the rhetorical and aesthetic program worked out by the *tlamatinime,* a correspondence was revealed linking the human personality, poetic structures, and the divine foundation of the universe together, through the use of this language art. In the moment when the speaker or artist truly expressed his or her heart in flower and song, the inner self was deified or filled with divine energy. This achievement meant that poetry and the human personality became linked to the divine duality above. The most profound truth—the reliable foundation of the cosmos—was the Lord and Lady of Duality, who were beyond "all time, beyond the heavens in Omeyocan." As with our discussion of the cosmos and human body, so with the Lord of Duality and the language of duality—the power and truth of celestial forces could be encapsulated in the spoken word.

Huehuetlatolli

One of the most influential instruments for organizing human behavior were the *huehuetlatolli* or the Ancient Word. These rhetorical orations were florid, elegant, metaphorical speeches, which were memorized and presented at ceremonial occasions such as the coronation of a ruler, the entry of a youth into the *calmecac,* the work of a midwife, or a marriage ceremony. *Huehuetlatolli* were also utilized when nobles gathered every eighty days in a special setting to receive admonitions and instructions of how to conduct themselves in war and peace. In this way these ancient words instructed Aztec peoples on friendship, learning, aspects of beauty, and proper worship of gods.

Consider the beauty and tenderness expressed in this *huehuetlatolli* spoken by a midwife to a newborn baby. Note how this formal speech required in midwife training reflects the patterns of cosmos and human body as well as divine duality and human language:

> And when the baby had arrived on earth, then the midwife shouted: she gave war cries, which meant that the little woman had fought a good battle, had become a brave warrior, had taken a captive, had captured a baby.
>
> Then the midwife spoke to it. If it was a male, she said to it: "Thou has arrived on earth, my youngest one, my beloved boy, my beloved youth."
>
> If it was a female, she said to it: "My beloved maiden, my youngest one, noblewoman, thou hast suffered exhaustion, thou hast become fatigued. Thy beloved father, the master the lord of the near, of the nigh, the creator of men, the maker of men, hath sent thee: . . . My youngest one! Perhaps thou wilt live for a little while! Art thou our reward? Art thou our merit? Perhaps thou wilt know thy grandfather, thy grandmothers, thy kinsmen, they lineage.
>
> In what way have thy mother, thy father Ome tecutli, Ome ciuatl, arrayed thee? In what manner have they endowed thee?"[19]

Some of the same elements of cosmovision appear in this opening passage of the *huehuetlatolli* spoken by a nobleman to his son exhorting him to sexual chastity.

> Thou who art my son, thou who art my youth, hear the words; place, inscribe in the chambers of thy heart the word or two which our forefathers departed leaving the old men, the old women, the regarded ones, the admired ones, and the advised one on earth. Here is that which they gave us, entrusted to us as they left the words of the old men, that which is bound, the well-guarded words. They left saying that the pure life is considered as a well-smoked, precious tur-

quoise: as a round, reedlike, well-formed, precious green stone. There is no blotch, no blemish. Those perfect in their hearts, in their manner of life, those of pure life—like these are the precious green stone, the precious turquoise, which are glistening, shining before the Lord of the Near, of the Close . . . For the Lord of the Near and Close has said, you are ordained one woman for one man. However, you are not to ruin yourself impetuously; you are not to devour, to gulp down the carnal life as if you were a dog.[20]

The force of these metaphors of affection, sexuality, and the gods combines to focus the listener on the main message: The gods befriend those who abstain from sex before and outside of marriage.

One of the Franciscan priests remarked around the middle of the sixteenth century that "no people loved their children more" than did the Aztecs. This love was also expressed in artistic speech. Rulers spoke to their daughters when they reached the age of discretion:

Here you are, my little girl, my necklace of precious stones, my plumage, my human creation, born of me. You are my blood, my color, my image . . .

Listen. Much do I want you to understand that you are noble. See that you are very precious, even while you are still only a little lady. You are a precious stone, you are a turquoise.[21]

Riddles

While Nahuatl language arts were florid, noble, and highly formal, they also contained a capacity for word pictures and wit. *Huehuetlatolli* included riddles, which were part of daily speech acts. Knowing the correct answer to riddles indicated that a person was from a good family. Note the ways that humankind and nature, cosmovision and human action, are related in these riddles:

What is a little blue-green jar filled with popcorn? Someone is sure to guess our riddle; it is the sky.

What is a warrior's hair-dress that knows the way to the region of the dead? Someone is sure to guess our riddle: it is a jug for drawing water from the well.

What is a mountainside that has a spring of water in it? Our nose.

What is it that goes along with foothills of the mountain patting out tortillas with its hands? A butterfly.

What is it that bends over us all over the world? The maize tassel.[22]

Finally let us review a series of proverbs used in social discourse, which reflect many of the religious dimensions discussed in this chapter.

Moxoxolotitlani = A page is sent. This is said about someone who is sent with a message and fails to return with an answer, or else does not go where he was sent. It is said for this reason. They say that when Quetzalcoatl was King of Tollan, two women were bathing in his pool. When he saw them he sent some messengers to see who they were. And the messengers just stayed there watching the women bathing and did not take him the information. Then Quetzalcoatl sent another of his pages to see who the bathers were and the same thing happened: he did not return with an answer either . . . From that time on they began, they started saying: A page is sent.

Niquauhtlamelaoa, tiquauhtlamelaoa = I am a fruitless tree, you are a fruitless tree. This is said when I study something but cannot learn it. It is exactly as if I were a fruit tree that bears no fruit.

Ipal nonixpatlaoa = Because of him my face becomes wide. This is said when someone's child—a boy or girl—or else someone's pupil, was well-taught, well-brought up.

And finally from the section on metaphors.

Tzopelic, auiyac = Sweet and fragrant. This was said about a city where there was prosperity and joy, or about a king who brought joy to the people.

In otitochtiac, in otimazatiac = You have turned into a rabbit, you have turned into a deer. This was said about someone who no longer lived at home. He no longer paid any attention to his father and mother but ran away when they wanted to correct him . . .

Yollotl, eztli = Heart and Blood
These words were said of chocolate because in the past it was precious and rare. The common people and the poor did not drink it. They also said it was deranging and it was thought to be like the mushroom, for it intoxicated people.[23]

With this sense of language and the sacred that we have gained, let us now turn to a different understanding of "heart and blood" equally as precious as chocolate but not nearly so rare.

Rites of Renewal and Human Sacrifice

We have explored four pervasive themes in Aztec religion as a means of understanding how their world was made, centered, and renewed: the tradition of Quetzalcoatl and Tollan; the cosmology of the human body; the Great Temple as *axis mundi,* and the art of language. All of these dimensions influenced the dynamics or splendid ceremonial cycles of Aztec religion, which involved different forms of sacrifice including human sacrifice, and wove together economic, political, military, and aesthetic institutions. The high priests who officiated and spoke at the major festivals involving human sacrifice at the Templo Mayor, for example, were called *quequetzalcoa* after the priest-king of Tollan. Now it is time to turn to two of these remarkable human celebrations: the New Fire Ceremony held only once every fifty-two years; and the festival of **Toxcatl** in honor of the awesome deity Tezcatlipoca, Lord of the Smoking Mirror. Each ceremony will be described in some detail and then interpreted within the context of Aztec religion as a whole.

The New Fire Ceremony

On a morning in the middle of November 1507 a procession of fire priests with a captive warrior "arranged in order and wearing the garb of the gods" processed out of the city of Tenochtitlan toward the ceremonial center on the Hill of the Star. During the days prior to this auspicious night the populace of the Aztec world participated together in the ritual extinction of fires, the casting of statues and hearthstones into the water, and the clean sweeping of houses, patios, and walkways. In anticipation of this fearful night women were closed up in granaries to avoid their transformation into fierce beasts who would eat men, pregnant women would put on masks of maguey leaves, and children were punched and nudged awake to avoid being turned into mice while asleep. For on this one night in the calendar round of 18,980 nights the Aztec fire priests celebrated "when the night was divided in half": the New Fire Ceremony that ensured the rebirth of the sun and the movement of the cosmos for another fifty-two years. This rebirth was achieved symbolically through the heart sacrifice of a brave, captured warrior specifically chosen by the king. We are told that when the procession arrived "in the deep night" at the Hill of the Star the populace climbed onto their roofs. With unwavering attention and necks craned toward the hill they became filled with dread that the sun would be destroyed forever.

It was thought that if the fire could not be drawn, the demons of darkness would descend to eat human beings. As the ceremony proceeded the priest watched the sky carefully for the movement of a star group known as Tianquitzli or Marketplace, the cluster we call the Pleiades. As it passed through the meridian signaling that the movement of the heavens had not ceased, a small fire was started on the outstretched chest of a warrior. The text reads, "When a little fire fell, then speedily the priests slashed open the breast with a flint knife, seized the heart, and thrust it into the fire. In the open chest a new fire was drawn and people could see it from everywhere."[24] The populace cut their ears—even the ears of children in cradles, the text tells us—and "spattered their blood in the ritual flicking of fingers in the direction of fire on the mountain." Then the new fire was taken down the mountain and carried to the pyramid temple of Huitzilopochtli in the center of the city of Tenochtitlan, where it was placed in the fire holder of the statue of the god. Then messengers, runners, and fire priests who had come from everywhere took the fire back to the cities where the common folk, after blistering themselves with the fire, placed it in their homes, and "all were quieted in their hearts."

This dramatic performance is extraordinarily thick and complex with meanings related to astronomy, calendars, ritual theaters, human sacrifice, and even child rearing. It is a clear example of what we have called worldcentering and worldrenewing. What is especially instructive is that the New Fire Ceremony integrates two major ceremonial centers and two cycles of time in one ceremony. Worldcentering and worldrenewing are doubly expressed.

The New Fire Ceremony, also called the Toxiuhmolpilia, Binding of the Years, actually tied together two important but very different ceremonial centers: the Great Temple of Tenochtitlan and the Hill of the Star. This rare ceremony, seen only once in a human lifetime, begins in the capital when the ruler Moctezuma orders a captive warrior be found whose name contains the word *xiuitl,* meaning turquoise, grass, or comet, a symbolic name connoting precious time. The procession of priests and deity impersonators moves along a prescribed passageway, presumably seen and heard by masses of people before arriving at the Hill of the Star. (In another report of this ceremony we are told that Moctezuma had a special devotion and reverence for this hill and shrine.) Then, having walked the 20 kilometers and climbed the ceremonial hill, the group of priests and lords, sharing a heightened sense of expectation and fear, seeks another procession: the procession of the stars through the meridian. Once the procession of stars is recognized, the heart sacrifice is carried out, and new fire is lit amid universal rejoicing and bleeding. Then, in the primary action that links the two "centers," the fire is taken back to the Templo Mayor. Next, in what I see as the most meaningful social and symbolic gesture, messengers, priests, and runners who have "come from all directions" to Templo Mayor take the fire back to the towns and cities on the periphery, where it ignites the new fire or time periods locally. In this way all the lesser units of the society, with their local shrines, are illuminated by the new fire, which links them to both the capital and the sacred hill. The fiery display ignites the imperial landscape by linking up all the sacred spaces in the Aztec world.

Aztec time is also renewed in this ceremony. Mesoamerican life was organized by two major calendar rounds, a 365-day solar cycle and a 260-day ritual cycle. Both calendars were divided into months, which were marked by carefully choreographed ritual performances and processions involving different cults, priestly groups, and communities. Mesoamerican priesthoods interlocked these cycles together, noting that all the possible interactive combinations became exhausted after 18,980 days or every fifty-two years. The end of this great cycle marked a point of cosmological crisis and transition. The New Fire Ceremony, focused on the heart sacrifice of a captive warrior, functioned to renew the beginning of these cycles for another fifty-two years. The power of this renewal came from two forces: the heart (*teyolia*) of humans and a new fire, which was ignited in the "hearth" created by the heart's extraction. When we remember divine forces were believed to reside in the human heart—and that the *teyolia* was believed to rise into the Sky of the Sun upon the death of a warrior—we can understand *what they believed they were accomplishing in this otherwise strange ceremony.* The Sun and celestial dynamics, or time, was being renewed from the gift of the *teyolia* that was being returned to the divine beings above.

Toxcatl: The Festival for Tezcatlipoca

Human sacrifice was not a random or occasional ritual practice: It took place in the Aztec world every month. Given what we have already studied about cosmology and the human body, and the New Fire Ceremony, we should now be able to understand—regardless of our sense of discomfort—the meaning and purpose of these rituals, described so shockingly by Díaz del Castillo at the beginning of this chapter. In order to further understand the meaning of human sacrifice in Aztec terms, let us look at one of the yearly festivals, Toxcatl.

Toxcatl was celebrated in honor of the "god of gods," Tezcatlipoca (Lord of the Smoking Mirror), one of the four creator gods who ordered the cosmos. The central act was the sacrifice of a captive warrior chosen for his perfect physical features. This youth was ritually changed into a *teotl ixiptla,* or image of the god, who paraded for one year throughout the Aztec city. At the end of the year the impersonator of Tezcatlipoca was sacrificed on top of a pyramid/temple, when his heart was extracted and offered to the sun. The impersonator was beheaded and his skull displayed on the skull rack in the ceremonial courtyard.

Let us consider the following stages of this ritual as described directly in the text.

The Aztec priests chose the most attractive physical male from a group of enemy warriors. There was a ritual prescription for the body type, as this excerpt shows.

> Indeed he who was thus chosen was . . . of good understanding, quick, of clean body, slender . . . long and thin, . . . like a stone column all over . . .
>
> Indeed it became his defect if someone were exceedingly tall. The woman said to him, "Tall fellow; tree-shaker; star gatherer."

A litany of detailed physical characteristics outline the type of human body needed for the ceremony:

> He who was chosen as impersonator was without defects. He was like something smoothed, like a tomato, like a pebble, as if sculptured in wood, he was not curly haired, curly headed . . . He was not rough of forehead; he had not pimples on his forehead. He did not have a forehead like a tomato: he did not have a baglike forehead. . . . he was not swollen cheeked; he was not of injured eyes; he was not of downcast face; he was not flat-nosed, not crooked nosed, but his nose was averagely placed . . . He was not thick lipped, he was not big lipped, he was not bowl lipped; he was not a stutterer, he did not speak a barbarous language. He was not buck-toothed, he was not yellow toothed, he was not ugly toothed, he was not rotten toothed, his teeth were like sea shells; they lay well, they lay in order . . . he was not fat, he was not big bellied, he was not of protruding navel, he was not of hatched shaped navel, he was not of wrinkled stomach, he was not of hatchet shaped buttocks, he was not of flabby buttocks.[25]

A post conquest depiction of human sacrifice from the Codex Magliabechiano. *The victim is held over the sacrificial stone while a priest cuts his heart out with a flint knife. Once the heart is removed, the victim is thrown down the steps of the temple. The divine power in the heart ascends into the sky. (Courtesy of University of California Press, Berkeley.)*

We see here the prime importance of the human body in the ritual of Toxcatl. The perfect container of divine energy is being chosen in recognition of Tezcatlipoca's status as a high god. After this individual is chosen he goes through a formal training period in the art of flower carrying, flute playing, speech arts, and whistle blowing in order to appear as the perfect image of Tezcatlipoca on earth. The impersonator and a specially trained guard/entourage of servants roam freely throughout the city for one year, showing the populace the living image of Lord of the Smoking Mirror. At the appointed time he is taken before the king Moctezuma and adorned with lavish cloaks, gifts, and luxuries, transforming the appearance of the impersonator into that of the living god. Following more public display the impersonator is given four wives, who are impersonating goddesses of agriculture, with whom he apparently has orgiastic sexual relations for twenty days prior to this sacrifice. Then he sheds his luscious ornaments in various places and his hair is cut into the style of a seasoned warrior.

With his deified wives he visits, dances, and sings at four ceremonial precincts, distributing food and gifts to the commoners before departing from the women and processing to the temple of Tlacochcalco. The text reads,

> He ascended by himself, he went up of his own free will, to where he was to die. As he was taken up a step, as he passed one step, there he broke, he shattered his flute, his whistle.
>
> And when he had mounted all the steps, when he had risen to the summit, then the offering priests seized him. They threw him upon his back on the sacrificial stone; then one of them cut open his breast; he took his heart from him, he also raised it in dedication to the sun. . . . But his body they did not roll down; rather, they lowered it. And his severed head they strung on the skull rack.[26]

In the extraordinary treatment given to Tezcatlipoca's living image on earth, we see the integration of a number of major elements of Aztec religion. The sacrificial victim is a captured warrior, as in the case of the mythical sacrifice at Coatepec. In this ceremony more than just the divine forces in the heart are released into the cosmos. Because the impersonator is Tezcatlipoca, the *tonalli* embedded in the skull of the perfect warrior is also offered as a gift to the god. Second, we see the importance of artistic display in the music, costume, rhetoric, and poise of Tezcatlipoca. He is a living

example of "flower and song," the divine truth on earth. The ceremony ends with the following statement of "truth on earth."

> And this betokened our life on earth. For he who rejoiced, who pos-
> sessed riches, who sought, who esteemed our lord's sweetness, his
> fragrance—richness, prosperity—thus ended in great misery. Indeed
> it was said: "No one on earth went exhausting happiness, riches,
> wealth."[27]

In this remarkable ceremony we are seeing the Aztec conception
of the perfect life and ideal death of the warrior displayed for all to
see as he parades, sings, plays music, and is sacrificed in public.

It is often asked whether sacrificial victims voluntarily surrendered themselves in the manner described here. Sources reveal that
in some cases the warriors attempted to escape during the ceremonies. We also know that victims fainted from fear as they approached the top of the temple. In other cases it appears that some
deity impersonators, especially women, did not know that they
were soon to be ritually killed. But it is also evident that, as in the
festival of Toxcatl, some impersonators surrendered willingly, even
with courageous displays of devotion to the sacrificial destiny. They
believed that their hearts and minds would, like Quetzalcoatl, be
transformed into eternal forces living in the heavens. This is perhaps the meaning of the claim that Tenochtitlan "is the foundation of heaven . . . where no one fears to die in war."

CHAPTER IV

Maya Religion: Cosmic Trees, Sacred Kings, and the Underworld

'The dawn has approached, preparations have been made, and morning has come for the provider, nurturer, born in the light, begotten in the light. Morning has come for humankind, for the people of the face of the earth,' they said. It all came together as they went on thinking in the darkness, in the night, as they searched and they sifted, they thought and they wondered.
Popul Vuh[1]

In 1949 Alberto Ruz, the chief excavator of the Temple of the Inscriptions at the Maya city of Palenque (4th–9th centuries CE), deduced that the floor of the rear hall concealed something below. He lifted several huge polished floor stones and discovered a steep staircase leading downward and packed with tons of stone rubble. Three years later in 1952, after arduous and careful work, Ruz opened for the first time in more than one thousand years the fabulous tomb of the Maya king Pacal (Lord Shield), who had ruled for sixty-eight years until his death in 683 CE.

In the center of the tomb stood the sarcophagus of Pacal, whose remains were found within, covered with remnants of a jade mask, necklaces, ear spools, rings, and a collection of jade and mother of pearl ornaments. On the walls and floors around the sarcophagus were reliefs of stucco, pottery vessels, stuccoed portrait heads, and the corpses of six sacrificial victims probably sacrificed on the occasion of Pacal's funeral. After the crypt was sealed a hollow miniature

Carved from a single slab of limestone, this lid covered the tomb of Lord Pacal, who ruled Palenque for sixty-four years. It depicts the cosmos at the moment of his death, as he descends down the world tree into the underworld. Sarcophagus Lid, Temple of the Inscriptions, Palenque, Chiapas, Mexico, CE 684. (Courtesy, Editions Albert Guillot, 4 rue de Seze, Lyon, France.)

stairway made of thin slabs of stone leading upward from the crypt to the upper Temple floor provided for communication between Pacal and the upper world. But the most revealing part of the tomb was the intricately carved sarcophagus lid, measuring more than twelve by seven feet, which depicted the image of the Maya cosmos and Pacal's movement through it. It consisted in part of

- a fantastic tree, decorated with jewels, mirrors, bloodletting bowls, dragons, bones, and a celestial bird on top
- the image of Pacal, with a small bone attached to his nose at the moment of death, falling
- into the gaping jaws of the Underworld, pictured as two huge skeletal dragons joined at the chin to form a U-shaped opening representing the passage to Xibalba. Other underworld symbols decorate the lid. Around the sides of the sarcophagus were vertically carved images of Pacal's ancestors emerging from trees, and on the floor were
- five or six human sacrificial victims who had been killed when the tomb was sealed.

This interrelated imagery of tree, king, ancestor sacrifice, and the underworld tells us that

for the Maya, the world was a complex and awesome place, alive with sacred power. This power was part of the landscape, of the fabric of space and time, of things both living and inanimate and of the forces of nature—storms, wind, smoke, mist, rain, earth, sky and water. Sacred beings moved between the three levels of the cosmos, the Overworld which is the heavens, the Middleworld where humans live and the Underworld of Xibalba, the source of disease and death. The king acted as a transformer through whom in ritual acts, the unspeakable power of the supernatural passed into the lives of mortal men and their works. The person of the king was also sacred. His clothing reflected more than wealth and prestige: it was a symbolic array identifying rank, ritual context and the sacred person he manifested.[2]

This chapter will explore the awesome, sacred world of the Maya, which was centered on the flowering cosmic tree and the lives of royal families and their intimate ties to ancestors. We will also see, following our general concern for "world renewal," how various means of sacrifice and mythical and spiritual journeys through the underworld revitalized the Maya cosmos. We will see that just as the bone attached to Pacal's nose symbolizes a large seed or his regeneration, so the Maya believed that it was possible, through cosmo-magical struggles to overcome death and experience a spiritual future including return visits to the earthly level. In this way we can, like King Pacal, descend into the rich world of meaning that filled the Maya cosmos.

The Lost Civilization of the Maya

There has always been a mystique surrounding the jungle civilization of the Classic Maya, who flourished between 200 and 900 CE. Whether referred to in a number of books as the "Lost Civilization," or superficially depicted in movies as treasure houses for *Raiders of the Lost Ark* or *Star Wars* rebel bases, the lost Maya have been like screens upon which modern cultures have projected their own ideas about noble savages. In the works of novelists, scholars, and travel agencies of the early twentieth century they have been portrayed as the great exception to the patterns of settlement and human character found in other ancient civilizations. This process of making the Maya so exceptional began, in part, with the discovery of the ruins of Copan in the Honduran jungle by the traveling diplomat John L. Stephens and the artist Frederick Catherwood. Stephens wrote after struggling through the jungle-covered site,

> We sat down on the very edge of the wall and strove in vain to penetrate the mystery by which we were surrounded. Who were the people that built this city? In the ruined cities of Egypt, even in the long lost Petra, the stranger knows the story of the people whose vestiges are around him. America, say historians, was peopled by savages: but savages never reared these structures, savages never carved these stones . . . There were no associations connected with the place; none of those stirring recollections which hallow Rome, Athens, and "the world's great mistress" on the Egyptian plain; but architecture, sculpture, and painting, all the arts which embellished life, had flourished in this overgrown forest; orators, warriors and statesmen, beauty, ambition and glory had lived and passed away, and none knew that such things had been, or could tell of their past existence.[3]

These attempts to relate in one way or another the Maya cities with the great civilizations of the so-called Old World continued on in the nineteenth century and received a fantastic series of twists by the French photographer and explorer Augustus Le Plongeon, who did archaeological and photographic work in Yucatan between 1873 and 1884. Le Plongeon made a splendid photographic record of Maya ritual buildings, iconography, and sculpture, which demands universal respect today. But at the same time he developed fantastic theories about the original homeland of the Maya and of their cultural achievements. He argued in a series of publications that the Maya were descendants of the lost civilization of Atlantis and the founders of Egyptian and Babylonian civilizations. Later scholars argued the reverse, that the Maya had migrated from Egypt. It appears unlikely that there were any such migrations of cultural significance. Le Plongeon also believed that the Maya's hieroglyphics indicated that they had prophesied that one day the telegraph would be used!

A more modern vision of the Maya, developed during the first half of the twentieth century, persisted until thirty years ago. In this vision the Maya were presented in popular and academic books as being a peaceful civilization directed by priests who were intense stargazers and mathematical geniuses. It was also believed that they lived in settlements that were neither village nor city but some vague utopian form of human habitation. This image was often put forth with glee in the face of the Aztec portrait of thundering warriors with bloodthirsty intentions celebrated on pyramids of carnage and cruelty. The more general claim was that the Maya were an ideal civilization unique in world history.

This view of the lost Maya ideal was shattered in the 1946 discovery of the murals at the ceremonial center of **Bonampak** in southern Mexico. Three rooms containing elaborate paintings presented a narrative of Maya life as a society dedicated to warfare and public human sacrifice under the direction of a royal family involved in the investiture of a prince into the line of succession to the sacred royal throne. Further research revealed that the Maya lived in socially stratified societies spatially organized around monumental ceremonial centers directed by sacred priesthoods who shared immense power with royal families in whom the ultimate authority, on earth, resided. It has become clear that Maya life was animated by an obsession with lineage. In a number of cases these ceremonial cities contained three distinctive zones of habitation: a central zone, adjacent to the ceremonial core where the elite class lived; a closely surrounding residential zone with mixed elites and commoner homes; and a peripheral residential area, where commoners and agricultural workers resided. This spatial layering was accompanied with distinctive degrees of access to status, goods, and power. A very serious collaborative effort by scholars from various disciplines has developed this more realistic and yet fascinating view of Maya religion and society.

The Maya region has been divided by scholars into three subregions: the southern subregion of the Guatemala highlands and the Pacific coast; the central subregion of northern Guatemala and its adjacent lowlands and the Peten region of Guatemala; and the northern region of the Yucatan Peninsula north of the Peten.

The greatest Maya achievements took place in the central and northern subregions in a number of major and minor ceremonial centers during what archaeologists have designated the Classic Period. For practical purposes scholars have divided Maya history in particular (Mesoamerican history in general) into three major phases. The Formative Period (1800 BCE–100 CE) was characterized by the gradual rise of complex ceremonial centers and the appearance of monumental architecture. During this period hieroglyphic writing and calendrics, the induction of social stratification, short and long-distance trade routes, and the first outlines of political statehood developed in several areas. A few large-scale city-states organized by dominant cities such as El Mirador and Kaminaljuyú appear to have emerged toward the end of this period. New evidence indicates that the Long Count calendar, which eventually flourished in the Classic Period, was developing in the southern regions during this Formative Period. The Classic Period (200 CE–900 CE), which we are focusing on in this chapter, resulted in the maturation of these processes, including the proliferation of ritual and solar calendrical systems, sizable agricultural bureaucracies, and the emergence in several areas of intense, even brutal, competition between powerful ceremonial centers. In the Maya area, however, the pattern of state organization was generally restricted to a series of competing city-states, a few of which extended strong religious and political influence to other regional sites.

The Post-Classic Period covers the development of the Maya world down to the conquest. It is quite astonishing that the greatest Maya achievements took place in the forests and jungles of Guatemala and Mexico. The extraordinary range of religious forms can only be illustrated here through reference to a handful of major sites.

Many of the Maya ceremonial centers were architectural wonders containing steep pyramid temples, large and small standing stelae or stone columns with writing and images, ball courts, palaces, and stairways. Throughout these ceremonial centers was spread a writing system that has puzzled and frustrated scholars for four hundred years. A major breakthrough in reading the Maya texts occurred in 1960, when Tatiana Proskouriakoff revealed that Maya inscriptions could be read and that they were primarily historical accounts of lives, families, and deaths of Maya royalty though not without astronomical references. Due to an unusual cooperative effort among Maya specialists we are gaining an in-depth understanding of the dynastic histories and sacred cosmologies of such beautifully built cities as Palenque, Caracol, Copán, Tikal, Dos Pilas, Yaxchilán, and many others. It has been discovered that the Maya told their histories and cosmologies in "pictorial programs" carved and painted on buildings throughout their ceremonial centers. One cosmic symbol that organizes and renews the Maya world is the sacred, flowering tree.

The Cosmic Tree

In order to get a good focus on the Maya cosmic tree we must first discuss the general idea of the cosmic tree. Then we will return to the ceremonial center of Palenque, where the cosmic tree is depicted in various, fantastic forms in a number of ceremonial buildings.

The Maya world was covered with vegetation. The people survived and prospered, in large part, through agricultural cultivation and production. We can tell from the rich images and clusters of images in Maya art that the people shared an agricultural mentality, that is, they were deeply committed to the continual regeneration of the plant world. This mentality springs from the insight that agriculture is not just a profane skill, but that it deals with powers and life forces that dwell in the seeds, furrows, rain, and sunshine. Human society and the agricultural process are viewed as set within and dependent upon the dramatic and tense cosmic cycles that insure the vital process of plant fertilization, ripening, harvest, decay, death, and rebirth. The forces in the plants, land, and rains are viewed as sacred forces, which reveal themselves in dramatic and critical moments that are never to be taken for granted. In fact the Maya not only considered the plants and seeds as in need of regeneration, but the entire cosmos depended on various processes of rebirth.

We can see the pervasive power of an agricultural mentality in the names and attributes of certain Maya gods. For instance, Itzamna was one of the most powerful Classic Maya gods associated with both the earth and sky, represented with reptilian features combining crocodile, lizard, and snake. He was the source of life-nurturing rains that produced the abundance of the Maya fields and forest. Another fertility force was Ah K'in, the sun who represented not only the forces of warmth that insured the reappearance of plant life, but also the threatening droughts. In the latter case Ah K'in was appeased to avoid agricultural disaster. All the Maya, but especially the peasants, worshiped the Chacs, who were associated with the four world directions from which flowed the rain that nurtured the fields and the trees. Equally important were the maize gods, who lived in the everpresent *milpas* or cornfields that surrounded the Maya ceremonial centers.

In the great myth of creation, recorded in the Quiché Maya book *Popul Vuh* or *Book of Council,* the cosmos is created in an agricultural style. At the beginning of time the gods created an abundant world of vegetation after they asked about the sky-earth (world):

> How should it be sown, how should it dawn? . . . Let it be this way, think about it: this water should be removed, emptied out for the formation of the earth's own plate and platform, then comes the sowing, the dawning of the sky-earth . . .
>
> And then the earth arose because of them, it was simply their word that brought it forth. For the forming of the earth they said "Earth." It arose suddenly just like a cloud, like a mist, now forming, unfolding. Then the mountains were separated from the water, all at once the great mountains came forth. By their genius alone, by

their cutting edge alone they carried out the conception of the
mountain-plain, whose face grew instant groves of cypress and pine.[4]

This cosmic sowing and dawning provides the model for all
subsequent creations, innovations, and changes. In Maya mythology seeds are sown in the earth to dawn as plants; celestial bodies
are sown beneath the earth to dawn in their rising; humans are
sown in mothers' wombs to dawn into life; and the dead are sown
in the underworld to dawn as sparks of light in the darkness. The
world's first dawn, brought forth through the sun's rays, emerges
with the appearance of the planet Venus:

> And here is the dawning and sowing of the Sun, Moon, and Stars,
> and Jaguar Quitze, Jaguar Night, Mahucutah, and True Jaguar
> were overjoyed when they saw the daybringer. It came up first. It
> looked brilliant when it came up since it was ahead of the sun.[5]

In the Maya theory of creation, reflected in this pattern of the
first and therefore subsequent sunrises, the world is in a continual
process of sowing, and dawning (sprouting). The Maya conceived
of this process as "a long performance," which hopefully would
never end.

It is important to remark that this pattern of birth, death, and
rebirth reflects a worldwide pattern of religious symbolism in
which the cosmos is likened to a cosmic tree or some form of vegetation. The cosmic tree symbol, which is found in China, Egypt,
Mesopotamia, Africa, and other Native American cultures, represents in Mircea Eliade's words the "world as a living totality, periodically regenerating itself and, because of this regeneration,
continually fruitful, rich and inexhaustible."[6] The Maya version of
this worldwide symbolism is still a vital symbolic force among
some Maya, including the **Tzutujil** Mayas of present-day Guatemala. One of the most powerful images of daily and ritual life is
expressed in the words *kotsej juyu ruchiliev* or "flowering mountain earth." The entire terrestrial level inhabited by animals, plants,
and humans is viewed as a tree or maize plant that repeatedly
sprouts, blossoms, wilts, dies, and is reborn. According to Tzutujil
mythology there existed a god in the form of a tree before the creation began. This tree stood in the center of chaos. This god-tree
became pregnant with potential life as the creation of the universe
approached. It began to flower and grew, in the form of fruit, one

of everything that was to exist in the created world. Robert Carlsen and Martin Prechtel, who have learned the religious patterns of the contemporary Maya, summarize this process:

> Not only were there gross physical objects like rocks, maize and deer hanging from the branches of this tree, there were also such elements as lightning and even individual segments of time. Eventually this abundance became too much for the tree to support, and the fruit fell. Smashing open, the fruit spread their seeds, and soon there were numerous seedlings growing at the foot of the old tree. The great tree provided shelter to the young "plants," nurturing them, until finally the old tree was itself crowded out by the new. Since then, this tree has existed as a stump at the center of the world. This stump is what remains of the original "Father/Mother" (Te Tie Te Tixel), the source and purpose of life. Moreover, this tree stump constitutes that force which allows the world to flower anew. In this way the world was created . . .[7]

A number of fascinating details about the Maya Cosmic tree of the Classic Period reflect this view. Let us return to the image on Pacal's sarcophagus and concentrate on the Classic Maya image. (See figure, p. 93.)

The Maya tree typically, as in this case, is rooted in the underworld, has its trunk in the middleworld, and its high branches or top ascending into heaven or the upperworld. In this way it unites, through a vertical column, the cosmos and its diverse powers, forces, deities, and dangers. It was believed that the souls of the dead—in this case the soul of Pacal—descend and ascend along the axis provided by the tree. Characteristically the Maya tree has a supernatural bird perched on the top symbolizing the celestial realm of the universe.

In the case of Pacal's tomb, the tree emerges out of the underworld shown as two gaping skeletal jaws of the earth. Pacal is seated on the head of the Four-Sided Sun Monster, which is shown at the moment of sunset. Like Pacal the sun is descending into the night of Xibalba, the underworld. The meaning is also that Pacal, like the sun, will emerge from the underworld in a new form. The trunk of the tree is marked with mirror symbols, indicating that it has brilliance and power—or in Maya religion, sacred energy. At the top of the trunk (1) is a bloodletting bowl outlined with beads of blood. At the edges of the branches (2) are two more bloodletting bowls with square-nosed dragons with jade cylinders and beads lining their mouths, signifying that they are very sacred. These symbols have cosmic meaning. The jeweled dragons at (3) represent the heavens, while the skeletal dragons below (4) represent the world of death into which Pacal is descending.

The earthly level is represented by the double-headed serpent bar (5) wrapped around the branches of the world tree, from which fleshed dragon heads with open mouths emerge. These fleshed beings represent the earthly level where the human community organized around the ruler (symbolized by the double-headed serpent bar) is situated.

But this entire scene is in motion. Pacal is pictured at the moment of his fall into the underworld, the sun is sinking below the horizon, and the tree is alive with its miraculous energies and beings. This dynamic motion is also present in the ancestral portraits carved on the side of the sarcophagus. Pacal's ancestors are depicted as emerging with a fruit tree from a crack in the earth, signifying the complementary action of dying and rising, descent and ascent.

One of the most impressive aspects of the art and architecture of Palenque is the series of cosmic trees that adorn the Temple of the Foliated Cross and the Temple of the Cross. Each has a significant variation on the themes discussed above. The central image of the Temple of the Foliated Cross, for example, depicts the cosmic tree rising from a symbol of the ancestral abode. The central tree is actually a composite of the four sacred trees associated with one of the four directions of the universe. The tie between agriculture and humans is signified when the tree is transformed into a flowering corn plant. However, instead of producing ears of corn, the plant creates the heads of young males, which rest on the leaves. For in Maya thought, the beauty of young males may symbolize the ripe maize, which may in turn represent the young male ruler ascending (or sprouting) to the throne.

This pattern of corn and rebirth reflects another major theme in Maya thought, that is, the meaning of the sun as a divine regenerative force. This pattern has recently been illuminated in Gary Gossen's *Chamulas in the World of the Sun,* a study of a Tzotzil-speaking Maya community in southern Mexico. The oral tradition of this contemporary Maya community reveals that the sun deity is the major symbol connecting ideas of order, verticality, heat, light, maleness, age, and renewal. All Chamula rituals include references to the great drama of the sun's ascent into the cosmos. It is possible that these contemporary patterns reflect ideas that animated the classic Maya ceremonial world.

The symbol of the *axis mundi* is associated with many of the major elements of the religious world: agriculture, warfare, heaven, ancestors, the underworld, and kingship. The most powerful earthly being associated with the cosmic tree was the king, who was considered the human *axis mundi* of the Maya world.

Sacred Kingship

We have seen throughout our study of Mesoamerican religion that human beings were "centers" of religious power and prestige. The human body, warriors, priests, and especially individuals such as Topiltzin Quetzalcoatl, Nezahualcoyotl, and Pacal oriented human consciousness and provided immediate contact with the sacred. The highest expression of human sacrality in the Maya world was in the royal families and especially the supreme rulers who descended from sacred lineages. Not only did their bodies contain divine fire and energy, but their clothes, bloodlines, paraphernalia, and especially their ritual actions brought the divine into the terrestrial level of existence. To understand this extraordinarily powerful type of individual in Maya religion we will look at the general nature of sacred kingship and then turn to two dimensions of Maya kings: the royal clothes, and rites of bloodletting expressive of royal authority.

One way to appreciate the awesome influence of Maya kings is to ask, "What were they the center *of?*" The answer is both simple and complex. Kings or rulers were the center of everything in heaven and earth. They were the living *axis mundi,* the embodiment of tradition and the symbol of totality. In broader terms rulers, especially in urban societies, stood at the center of an "ecological complex" consisting of five dimensions of society: cultivation of the natural environment, movements and life-styles of the human population, developments of technology, conflict, and warfare, and developments of social status and structure. The king was the supreme authority who, with the advice of his ruling family and council, directed the work of intensive agriculture and trading; the ceremonial cycles that attracted peoples to the city; the use and innovations in arts, crafts, tool making, and weaponry; initiated the outbreak of conflicts with other communities; and regulated the rewards for the maintenance of social status. All this was managed from the supremely sacred location of the temple communities at the heart of society. The sources of the authority to carry out the immense power of kingship were the cosmic beings and especially ancestors, in the Maya case, who became incarnate in the body, blood, actions, and costume of the ruler.

This pattern of rulership was present, in a particular form, in Maya society. It was based on four basic assumptions lodged in the Maya worldview. First, it was believed that a powerful cosmic order permeated every level and dimension of the world from the heavens, through the clouds, through the things on the earth and into the realms of the underworld. Second, it was believed that human society would be stable as long as it operated as a microcosm or approximate imitation of the cosmic order constructed by the gods. Third, it was the role of the sacred kings to align the social world of the humans with the supernatural world of the gods. Fourth, the king had to demonstrate through ritual his line of descent from the first ancestor who was the source of sacrality. The main technique for Maya kings to bring the social and supernatural world into alignment was ritual action.

Maya Kings Dressed to Kill

Maya rulers were called Mah K'ina (Great Sun Lords), or Ahau (Lord). Unlike the social pattern in Aztec culture, where competing city-states gave way to imperial centers such as Teotihuacan and Tenochtitlan, Maya culture tended to maintain regional centers of power such as Palenque, Yaxchilán, Copán, and Quiriguá. The result was a series of powerful local or regional rulers in periodic competition with other city-states. We know of such rulers as Smoke Jaguar, Yax Pac (First Dawn), Kakukpacal (Fire Is His Shield), Shield Jaguar, Two-Legged Sky. What we know about these rulers and their ritual techniques comes primarily from the fabulous art, writing, and architectural traditions imprinted in the surviving ceremonial centers, pottery, and sculpture. Let us turn to a consideration of the royal costume to see how the supernatural and the king became so closely identified.

The Great Sun Lords were sacred, in part, because of the clothes they wore. They were carefully and richly adorned with arrays of brilliant and colorful objects made of wood, cloth, feathers (quetzal, macaw, parrot), shells, and stones (jade, pyrite, obsidian), which were transformed into belts, pectorals, knee guards, bracelets, and large undulating headdresses often in zoomorphic styles. They also carried sacred bundles filled with objects representing the presence of the divinities. Once arrayed with these prestigious and potent objects, they hardly appeared human at all. They represented a sacred presence organized by cosmic symbols of very high status. Embedded in their costumes were images of myths, gods, and spatial domains. These royal persons were living cosmograms designed to inspire awe, respect, and obedience.

Let us focus on one typical, extravagant image of a ruler dressed, literally, to kill. The image of the ruler of Dos Pilas appears in frontal position with his head turned to the left. Our general impression is that we are looking at a human being who has been transformed into a fantastic series of circles, lines, waves, and images associated not only with high rank but also supernatural power. For instance the ruler has a fabulous, opulent headdress consisting of feathers, wood, jade, and beads organized by an animal image. The zoomorphic head (a) is mounted directly above the face and lacks a lower jaw, so that the ruler's head emerges from the mouth of the animal. In some cases rulers had several animal heads constituting their headdress associated with war or bloodletting, fertility, or kingship, according to the ritual occasion. These headdresses symbolized the intimate relations between the powers of these animals and the royal person who obtained and wielded these awesome forces. The ruler contains the powers of the god, as in the case of **Chac-Xib-Chac,** the god of war, sacrifice, and dancing.[8]

Let us focus our eyes on two other aspects of this image to see how ritual action involved kings in the practice of worldcentering and worldrenewing. When we move our eyes below the head (b) we see an intricately designed large, round pectoral with triple loops extending horizontally to cover the king's chest. These three

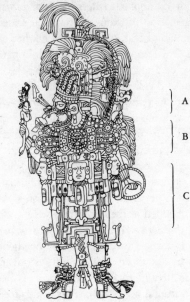

} A

} B

| C

This drawing of Stela 1 from Dos Pilas shows a Maya ruler at the time of his accession to the throne. His elaborate costume is complemented with the heads of sacrificial captives, plumes, and precious jewels. (Drawings courtesy of Linda Schele.)

loops indicated that the king was dressed as one of a group of immensely powerful gods who inspired and supported his actions. The idea is also that the powers of supernatural entities reside in the chest as well as the head of the king.

Below this (c) the ruler wears a knee-length apron with the image of a God, known only as God C, with a square-nosed serpent design framing both sides of his legs. This apron is a royal symbol of the cosmic tree and signifies that the king, like the symbolic tree we have just interpreted, was the center of the Maya cosmos. The king, like the flowering tree, is the central human image whose actions renew the world in ritual. The main ritual action that gave new life to the gods and agriculture was bloodletting. In the case of this king's costume imagery a number of elements are associated with the onset of warfare and the offering of captured warriors for sacrifice. This ruler is dressed to kill and offer blood.

Bleeding for a Vision of Regeneration

In order to understand the unusual practice of bloodletting we must place our discussion within the context of two important

Maya cultural patterns: reciprocity and rites of passage. Reciprocity was established by the Maya gods during their struggle to create human beings. Rites of passage is what the Maya do in order to periodically renew their relationship with the forces that created them.

Reciprocity

In the Maya world, as in many religious traditions, humans and gods have a relationship based on some form of mutual care and nurturance. The gods create humans, who are therefore in their debt. The ongoing existence of human life depends on the generous gifts of life, which the gods continue to dispense through children, germination, rain, sunshine, the supply of animals, and objects of power. But the gods are also dependent beings, at least in the Maya world. They depend on humans to care, nurture, acknowledge, and renew their powers.

The Quiché Maya story of creation reveals the character of this reciprocal relationship. The following excerpts come from the *Popul Vuh,* discovered and translated in Guatemala around 1702. Even though it was produced after the conquest it contains many myths and ritual traditions that relate to the time of Pacal and his precursors. Let's consider some opening passages that reveal the creative acts of the gods and the manner in which earthly existence depends on their power and generosity. These creative acts are the first step in the formation of reciprocity. We can also see some interesting parallels with Aztec creation stories.

This is the beginning of the Ancient Word, here in this place called Quiché. Here we shall inscribe, we shall implant the Ancient Word, the potential and source for everything done in the citadel of Quiché, in the nation of Quiché people.

> And here we shall take up the demonstration,
> revelation, and account of how things were put in
> shadow and brought to light
> by the Maker, Modeler, named Bearer, Begetter,
> Hunahpu Possum Hunahpu Coyote,
> Great White Peccary, Tapir,
> Sovereign Plumed Serpent,

> Heart of the Lake, Heart of the Sea,
> Maker of the Blue-Green Plate,
> Maker of the Blue-Green Bowl,

as they are called, also named, also described as

> the midwife, matchmaker
> named Xpiyacoc, Xmucane,
> defender, protector.
> twice a midwife, twice a matchmaker,

as is said in the words of Quiché. They accounted for everything—and did it, too—as enlightened beings, in enlightened words.[9]

In this opening section we see that the creation is likened to planting and sprouting or sowing and dawning, in the words of the text "things were put in shadow and brought to light." What was brought to light was a divine society made up of immensely powerful "enlightened beings" who made "everything."

The world was created as a great ritual action. In the words of the text, "It takes a long performance and account to complete the emergence of all the sky-earth." The world, in other words, is created both by a telling (account) and a doing (performance). This cosmos has order and structure for beings to dwell in. The sky-earth had

> the fourfold siding, fourfold cornering,
> measuring, fourfold staking,
> halving the cord, stretching the cord
> in the sky, on the earth,
> the four sides, the four corners.[10]

The beauty of this story continues when we are told of the "first eloquence," which describes the world before the gods decide to gather and create animals and humans.

There is not yet one person, one animal, bird, fish, crab, tree, rock hollow, canyon, meadow, forest. Only the sky alone is there; the face of the earth is not clear. Only the sea alone is there; the face of the earth is not clear. Only the sea alone is pooled under all the sky; there is nothing whatever gathered together. It is at rest; not a single thing stirs. It is held back, kept at rest under the sky.

Whatever there is that might be is simply not there; only the pooled water, only the calm sea, only it alone is pooled.[11]

In this primordial stillness the gods in the sky and the "Bearers, Begetters are in the water, a glittering light" speak and plan for the "dawn of life . . . How should it be sown, how should it dawn."

They decided to make trees, bushes, animals, and humans and set about to organize the terrestrial level. They were successful in all matters but one, the creation of humankind. Each of three attempts to create humans failed. And in the narrative of their attempts we see how *reciprocity* is intended in their creation of humans.

> Again there comes an experiment with the human work, the human design, by the maker, Modeler, Bearer, Begetter:
>
> "It must simply be tried again. The time for the planting and dawning is nearing. For this we must make a provider and nurturer. How else can we be invoked and remembered on the face of the earth? We have already made our first try at our work and design, but it turned out that they didn't keep our days, nor did they glorify us.
>
> "So now let's try to make a giver of praise, giver of respect, provider, nurturer," they said.[12]

Herein we see the reason for the creation of human life: so that the gods will have beings who can praise, respect, provide for, and nurture the gods. A short formula of this relationship can be stated, "We create your life so that you can praise, nurture, and call us into your community." The form of praising, respecting, and calling the gods into the Maya social world was, in part, bloodletting. This technique is part of a larger religious tradition humans use to fulfill their part of the bargain. It is referred to, in general terms, as "rites of passage."

Rites of Passage

Rites of passage are a category of rituals that mark the passage of a person through the life cycle, from one stage to another over time, from one role or social position to another, integrating the human and cultural experiences with biological destiny: birth, reproduction, and death. These rituals enable the individual to make a significant passage through a direct *experience* of the sacred and through *learning* about the human/divine relationship as defined by a particular culture. In Maya society there were rites of passage for all members of the society at birth, puberty, marriage, at significant moments in the agricultural year, on becoming a warrior or priest, and at death. But in Maya religion, rites of passage extended beyond the death of the individual to include moments of reintegration into the terrestrial world. The most powerful rite of passage was the accession to the throne of royal persons. What is special about the rite of accession to the office of ruler in Maya religion is that another type of "passage" was sought and achieved through bloodletting, namely, the passage of ancestors and supernatural beings into the world of the human. The *opening* or passageway for this passage was the wound in the human body and blood. This opening was especially crucial for lords seeking to become rulers. For it was through bloodletting that a real reciprocity was achieved. On the one hand the royal person was passing to a higher social and sacred status, that of the supreme ruler. On the other hand the gods were passing into the world of humans to be reborn. The Maya gave blood in order to receive a vision in which the gods and ancestors appeared in the world of the ceremonial center and in order to perceive the spiritual presence of their ancestors.

Though it may seem strange to modern readers, bloodletting was not strange or unusual in Maya culture. It was described in the mythology of various communities, part of the public rituals of everyday life, and central to the ritual actions of the upper classes. Bloodletting was done at the dedication of buildings and monuments, the birth of children, marriage ceremonies, all political events, moments of transition in the calendar, and at life cycle rituals. It has been called the "mortar of Maya life" because it not only signaled major transitions, it also integrated the levels of the cosmos and the social groups into a sense of wholeness. In order to gain more detail and understanding about bloodletting we will focus on two religious meanings of this ritual practice. The first is the religious meaning of female blood. The second is the religious meaning of subincision of penis perforation.

This sculptured relief is an extraordinary depiction of a Late Classic Maya bloodletting rite. A king, Shield Jaguar, stands next to his ritual partner, Lady Xoc, who is engaged in pulling a thorned rope through her mutilated tongue. Dressed in cosmic symbols, she sheds the precious blood to sustain the gods and celebrates the king's accession to the throne. Lintel 24, Yaxchilán, Chiapas, Mexico, 725 CE. (Photo © Justin Kerr, 1985. Courtesy of British Museum.)

We are fortunate to have a series of carved lintels from the ceremonial center of Yaxchilán that depict progressive scenes of a royal Maya woman, Lady Xoc, and the ruler Shield Jaguar participating in a bloodletting ritual. In the first scene we see the king, Shield Jaguar, holding a huge torch above his ritual partner, Lady Xoc. Both are dressed in exquisite costumes decorated with cosmic designs. Notable are the shrunken head of a past sacrificial victim on Shield Jaguar's headdress, the beaded necklace with its Sun God pectoral hanging from his neck, highback sandals made of jaguar pelts, and a cape with designs of the four world directions. Jade ornaments encircle his knees and wrists, and his loincloth carries the ancestral lineage emblem. The shrunken head signifies his role in nurturing the gods through sacrifice. Lady Xoc wears a fabulous *huipil* (blouse) woven in a diamond pattern with star designs and a skyband border symbolizing heaven and particular astronomical events. Her headdress is decorated with tassels and a head of the rain god Tlaloc out of which feathers spring. Most important she is pulling a thorn-lined rope through her tongue. The rope falls into a woven basket, which contains paper with spots of blood on it. Her cheeks have scroll designs signifying the blood she is giving to the gods.

This remarkable scene, which probably took place at night, is associated with another depicted on Lintel 25 from Yaxchilán. Looking at the image we can see Lady Xoc crouching down but looking up at the gaping mouth of a Vision Serpent, from which emerges a fully armed Tlaloc warrior. This fantastic serpent emerges from the bloodied paper and rope in the ritual plate on the floor. The Tlaloc image on the headdress is associated with bloodletting, war, and sacrifice in Maya mythology.

In these scenes of ritual bleeding and the appearance of a vision we may be able to gain insight into the meaning of female blood in Maya religion. More work still needs to be done on the symbolism and political importance of these scenes. But we can postulate that they may indicate that female blood, shed in this sacrificial manner opens the membrane between heaven and earth through which flow astronomical influences, the spirit of ancestors, and legitimate power for a ruler ascending the throne. It is not clear to scholars whether Lintel 25 depicts an ancestor emerging out of the mouth of the Vision Serpent or whether it is the birth of Shield Jaguar *as* a king.

Gods and Kings Bleeding for a Vision

As we might suspect, given our discussion of the Maya conception of reciprocity and rites of passage, gods also sacrificed their own blood and in some cases bled their genitals to stimulate visions. Maya art includes scenes in which gods create the ritual tradition of bleeding their penises. In one scene, on an elaborately carved pot, the Sun God who has performed a bloodletting rite is shown having a vision in the form of a Vision Serpent who spits out the Sun while another serpent in the same vision spits out the water of the underworld. In this vision the two halves of the cosmos, the sky and the earth, are visualized by the sacrificing deity. Within these cosmic spaces appear birds, plants, death, sacrifice, day and night. "The god's bloodletting vision is thus the whole cosmos."[13]

Maya art shows us that one of the body parts bled in order to stimulate visions was the royal penis. There are many images de-

picting rulers and their male relatives piercing their genitals in public and private settings. What can be the meaning of males giving
blood in this manner? Fortunately we have inscriptions associated
with some of these scenes suggesting that the Maya lords sought to
experience a *totality,* even a divine totality, by imitating the capacity of women to menstruate (bleed from their genitals) and to give
birth. In several cases the Maya kings are referred to as "mother of
the gods," who gives birth—that is, brings the gods into being on
a terrestrial level—through bloodletting. It is through the blood of
the king that he becomes both male ruler and female nurturer of
the Maya gods. This kind of giving, pain, and generosity was one
of the ultimate means to participate in a truly reciprocal relationship with divine forces.

The Calendar and the Regeneration of Time

At the beginning of this chapter we viewed the imagery of Pacal's
descent into the underworld. The symbolism of the seed on his
nose symbolized his potential for regeneration following an ordeal
of traveling through Xibalba. The journey through Xibalba was
one of the great themes of Maya religion that influenced commoner, warrior, farmer, weaver, and ruler.

Before we travel along with the Maya through the underworld
landscape and its ordeals, we need to describe and interpret one
other major ritual pattern of Maya culture, the sacred calendar.
The Maya calendar reveals two passions in Maya thought: the passion for pattern, and the passion for regeneration of time and life.
As we have implied throughout this study ancestors and ancestral
powers are considered the source for agriculture and even the regeneration of time. It is in the calendars of Maya culture that we
see inscribed these passions, which take the forms of mathematics
and ritual joined in one unit.

Unlike most other indigenous peoples of the Americas, the
Maya developed an elaborate writing system capable of recording
the range and meanings of their spoken language. Fortunately we
have abundant evidence of this writing system on the ball courts,
temples, stelae, stairways, codices, and pottery of the Classic Maya.
The typical presentation of this writing system combines written

texts, carved into the stone, with pictorial programs depicting ritual and political action. In this manner the viewer or reader had two sources of information about the scenes portrayed. In some cases the written texts told of events leading up to the pictorial scene in front of the viewer. Some Maya scholars have called these scenes with their inscriptions Maya "cartoons," because they contain frozen framed images with accompanying narrations.

Permeating almost all Maya writing and pictorial scenes are calendrical notations indicating to us that the Maya were deeply concerned to locate all events, especially period ending dates, within a cosmological framework designed to insure the regeneration of life. The Maya generally believed that the universe had passed through at least three previous ages, with the present age beginning on a date corresponding to 3114 BCE. Time was moving systematically toward the end of the present cycle on December 23, 2012 CE. In other words time past and time future were fixed into a discernible pattern that could be read *and* predicted. In addition to this nearly five-thousand-year cycle were a series of other cycles, which the Maya marked, celebrated, and sometimes feared in detail.

First the Maya observed a temporal cycle we call the Calendar Round, which covered a fifty-two-year period. It consisted of two different calendars interlocked and rotating. The first, called Tzolkin or sacred round, consisted of 260 days built up by giving one of twenty day names to each day in succession, and giving one of thirteen numbers to each day in succession resulting in a number and a day name for each day, for example, 4 Ahau. Each of the 260 days had a unique number and day combination. This was the basic ritual calendar utilized throughout Mesoamerica. This cycle, interacted with the Haab (Cycle of Rains) or Vague Year, which divided the observed solar year of 360 days built up into eighteen months of twenty days plus one month of five days. Thus 2 Pop would be the second day of the first month of the Seasonal Year, which was named Pop. The five-day month at the end was called Uayeb and considered hazardous. The Maya named their days according to the intermeshing of each calendar so that, for instance, the day 4 Ahau 2 Pop marked a day on both the longer and shorter calendars. These two interlocking calendars exhausted all possible combinations after 18,980 days or 52 Haabs when 4 Ahau 2 Pop would recur again. This marked the end of a significant time period and the regeneration of a new temporal order.

This system was common throughout much of Mesoamerica and was the guiding calendrical pattern when the Spaniards invaded Mesoamerica in the early sixteenth century. However, the religious sensibility for pattern and renewal within the flow of time was also expressed in another, much more elaborate Long Count calendar, which according to some scholars measured time along a spectrum of over nine million years. Maya monuments throughout the ceremonial centers of Palenque, Yaxchilán, Copán, Tikal, Quiriguá, Uaxactún, and many others are incised with Long Count notations marking the date of birth, marriages, bloodletting ceremonies, warfare, anniversaries, enthronements, deaths, and the emergence of royal persons from the underworld.

The Long Count system is based in a vigesimal count; that is, it has a base of twenty rather than the base of ten used by European civilization. Instead of taking the Vague Year as the basis for the Long Count, the Maya and other peoples employed the *tun,* a period of 360 days composed of eighteen divisions of twenty days each. Consider the spacious sense of time in the Long Count cycles, which include

1 *kin*	=	1 day
20 *kins*	=	1 *uinal* or 20 days
18 *uinals*	=	1 *tun* or 360 days
20 *tuns*	=	1 *katun* or 7,200 days
20 *katuns*	=	1 *baktun* or 144,000 days

Long count dates inscribed by the Maya on their monuments consist of the above cycles listed from top to bottom in descending order of magnitude, each with its numerical coefficient, and all to be added up so as the express the number of days elapsed since the end of the last great cycle, a period of thirteen *baktuns,* whose ending fell on the date 4 Ahau 8 Cumku. Thus a long count date conventionally written as 9. 10. 19. 5. 11. would be calculated as follows:

9 *baktuns*	=	1,296,000 days
10 *katuns*	=	72,000 days
19 *tuns*	=	6,840 days
5 *uinals*	=	100 days
11 *kins*	=	11 days

In sum, this is 1,374,951 days since the close of the last great cycle, reaching the Calendar Round position 10 Chuen 4 Cumku.[14] It is important to reiterate that the Maya had come to understand the concept of zero, which was necessary to perform calculations in this positional count.

At important divisions in this Long Count system the entire Maya world took time and gave significant effort to celebrate transitions and new beginnings. The Maya lords offered blood in public settings at the end of each *katun* or 7,200 days as well as at each five-year interval within this twenty-year period. In this and in every way the Maya marked time with sacred rituals in order to both locate themselves with the great cycle of the cosmos and regenerate their smaller cycles of agricultural, social, and cosmic changes. It now is clear that the reason the Maya added the Long Count to the calendar round system was because they took dynastic succession to be the foundation of their society. Great lengths of time became important when remembering long chains of ancestors.

Archaeoastronomy and the Maya

Intimately related to the Maya calendar was the careful alignment of particular buildings and ceremonies with the dramatic cycles and appearances of celestial bodies, including the moon, sun, Venus, and so on. Recently a new academic discipline called archaeoastronomy has made major strides in understanding the relationship between ancient Mesoamerican astronomy, the natural landscape, ceremonial buildings, and human life. Defined as "the interdisciplinary study of the practice of astronomy by ancient peoples using both the written and unwritten record," archaeoastronomy has shown how major temples, entire ceremonial centers, and the calendars that guided ritual and social life were dependent, in part, on astronomical events and patterns. Although there are many interesting examples of the interrelationship of ceremonial centers and astronomy in Mesoamerica, I will briefly summarize just one as reported in the work of Anthony Aveni.[15]

A principal idea in the archaeoastronomy of Maya religion is the idea of "axiality," or the major orientation of a ceremonial center or building with reference to the local culture's notion of cardinal directionality. The Maya city of Chichén Itzá, for instance, is laid out so that the oldest part of the city is aligned 11 to 14 degrees east of north. This orientation/layout appears to have some particular astronomical pattern as its key.

More specifically, archaeoastronomers have been able to determine that **special assemblages** or groups of buildings misaligned in relationship to other buildings often have some precise architectural connection to astronomy. In the Maya area there are a group of buildings known as "E-VII/sub" in a number of architectural sites. At Uaxactun this group consists of four buildings, including a large platform on the west side of a plaza, which faces three other buildings to the east. When a ritual specialist stood on the western platform looking east he would have observed summer and winter solstice sunrises appearing over the north and south buildings respectively and the equinox sunrise occurring over the middle building. In this way the entire complex becomes a solar observatory that tells the elites when to prepare the community at large for planting, harvesting, warfare, and other crucial events regulated by the solar year.

This pattern of Maya ceremonial architecture is an excellent example of how cosmovision, the parallelism between celestial and earthly cycles, became inscribed on the material world of the ceremonial center.

The Ordeals of Xibalba

Death is a fact of the life cycle. Religions the world over teach us that human beings have developed meaningful ways of overcoming death. The basic human stance, whether expressed in statements such as "Death Be Not Proud," or funerary rituals, or visions of paradise, has been a stance of defeating death through rituals of transformation. These rituals include rites of separation such as human burial or cremation. But they also include songs, imagery, and stories that express the hope and belief that some core dimension of the human continues to live on past death and is reborn into a spiritual or divinized community. This pattern of death and rebirth was particularly powerful in the Maya world where war, sacrifice, and a short lifespan were accepted patterns of destiny.

One of the elaborate ways in which the Maya expressed their hope and belief in a life after death and after the struggles of earthly existence was through the pattern of the heroic journey through the Underworld of Xibalba. (Xibalba was simultaneously the Place of Death and the Place of Regenerative Powers symbolized by the ancestral seeds and skulls, the symbols of fertility.) As in many other classic statements about the underworld, such as Dante's *Inferno*, the Maya heroes faced extraordinary ordeals that had to be overcome before emerging once more to see the heavens with their orderly rhythm.

The belief in another world, or underworld, is widespread in the history of religions. Often the underworld is a place of punishment, pain, and frightening beings, who test and overcome the spirits of the deceased. A common theme is the descent of a hero into a cave, earth monster, belly of a whale, or some other creature of the Abyss. The hero undergoes terrible ordeals, including being dismembered, paralysis through fear, face-to-face encounters with the lords of the dead, and other kinds of contests during which one's ultimate destiny is at stake. One of the goals of these ordeals is new knowledge about the mysteries of existence, the afterlife, and powers of rebirth. Ideally the hero, usually with the help of some friendly spirit, overcomes the lords of the underworld, re-emerges from the earth, and achieves immortality. In Mesoamerica, as we saw in the case of Quetzalcoatl, the hero who is reborn often takes the form of an ancestral spirit or becomes part of a celestial body (or maize plant or world tree) now fully integrated into the patterns of the heavens.

Fortunately we have full and partial written accounts of the Maya version of this pattern, which we saw so vividly in the image of Palenque's ruler Pacal, entering the underworld with the setting sun. The implication was that he would be regenerated with the rising sun. In works such as the *Chilam Balam of Tizimin, Chilam Balam of Chumayel,* and the *Popul Vuh* or *Book of Council,* we find valuable information about the Maya view of the cosmos and the powers that inhabit it. In the amazing narrative of the *Popul Vuh* we see the Maya underworld as a dangerous landscape where gods and human spirits struggle to deceive, trick, sacrifice, and overcome one another. In some ways the Maya underworld is a sarcastic replica of life on earth. In other ways Xibalba is a landscape of awesome, dangerous beings who usually have their way.

One of the most revealing episodes in the underworld described by the *Popul Vuh* is the contest, in the form of a sacred ball game, between the Hero Twins **Hunahpu** and **Xbalanque** and the Lords of Xibalba. In the narrative the Hero Twins are playing ball at the ball court where their father and uncle had played a generation before. These ancestors had been invited down into Xibalba (that is, they had died), where they had been defeated and destroyed by the lords of the underworld. Now, a generation later, the boys are playing a game and disturb the Lords of Death by stomping around and bouncing the ball loudly. One Death and Seven Death and the other lords summon them into the underworld to play a game and undergo great ordeals. The message reaches them: "In seven days they are to come here. We'll play ball. Their gaming equipment must come along; rubber ball yokes, arm guards, kilts. This will make for some excitement here . . . " The boys

> went down to Xibalba, quickly going down the face of cliff, and they crossed over the bottom of a canyon with rapids. They passed right through the birds—the ones called thorn birds—and then they crossed Pus River and Blood River, intended as traps by Xibalba. They did not step in, but simply crossed over on their blowguns and they went on over to the Cross roads. But they knew about the roads of Xibalba: Black Road, White Road, Red Road, Green Road.[16]

With the help of a mosquito the Twins learn the names of the Lords: One Death, Seven Death, House Corner, Blood Gatherer, Pus Master, Jaundice Master, Bone Scepter, Skull Scepter, Wing, Packstrap, Bloody Teeth, Bloody Claws. These lords put the Twins through a series of ordeals. First, they are placed in the Dark House and given an impossible challenge. They are given a torch and two cigars and told that they must return them unconsumed in the morning. The Twins take the tail of macaw birds, which look like torches to the sentries, and put fireflies on the tips of the cigars, giving the false appearance of having them lit all night.

Undefeated by this trial, the Twins are then placed in a series of houses on different nights, each one representing an ordeal. They are first tested in the Razor House and survive by persuading "each and every knife (to) put down its point." Then the Xibalbans put them in the Cold House, where "countless drafts, thick falling hail" threaten to freeze them to death. Through cunning they survive and "were alive when it dawned." Then they were placed in the Jaguar House, the "jaguar-packed home of jaguars," who threaten to eat them. They scatter bones before the jaguars, who wrestle over the bones, ignoring the Twins. Then they are placed in the Fire House, where they are only simmered instead of burned. The "Xibalbans . . . lost heart over this." Finally they are forced into the Bat House, where "monstrous beasts, their snouts like knives, the instruments of death" threaten to "finish them off at once." The Twins slept in their blowguns and avoided this horrible death.

One of the twins, Hunahpu, meets his death; but the other Twin figures out a way to resurrect him. In other words they learn the secret of overcoming death. Hunahpu peeks out of his blowgun, attempting to see the dawn, and is decapitated. The Xibalbans are delighted to see Hunahpu's head rolling on to the ball court. Xbalanque replaces it with a carved squash and the Twins, now one with a squash for a head, play ball with the Xibalbans. Through trickery Xbalanque retrieves the original head and rejoins it to Hunahpu's head, regenerating his human form.

The text reads, "They did whatever they were instructed to do, going through all the dangers, the troubles that were made for them, but they did not die from the tests of Xibalba, nor were they defeated by all the voracious animals that inhabit Xibalba."[17] Yet they realize that their death is inevitable in the underworld and instruct two helpful shamans to tell the Lords of Death to kill them in a certain fashion that will, unknown to the Xibalbans, lead to their rebirth and defeat of Death. The Lords burn the Hero Twins in an oven and grind their bones into powder, which is thrown into the water. "On the fifth day they reappeared . . . having germinated in the waters." The Twins reappear in the disguise of vagabonds "with rags before and rags behind" dancing the Dance of the Poorwill, the Dance of the Weasel, and the Dance of the Armadillo. Like tricksters they travel about performing miracles and dancing before the Xibalbans. The most impressive miracles include sacrificing a dog that revives, and burning a house that is not consumed.

Then the lord said to them: "Sacrifice my dog, then bring him back to life again," they were told.

"Yes," they said.

> When they sacrificed the dog
> he then came back to life.
> And that dog was really happy
> when he came back to life.

Then the Lords of Death insist that they carry out a human sacrifice and regenerate the victim.

> And they they took hold of a human sacrifice.
> And they held up a human heart on high.
> And they showed its roundness to the lords.

And now One and Seven Death admired it, and now that person was brought right back to life. His heart was overjoyed when he came back to life, and the lords were amazed.[18]

So amazed were the Lords that they commanded the distinguished Twins to sacrifice and regenerate themselves. So Hunahpu was sacrificed by Xbalanque. "His heart, dug out, was smothered in a leaf, and all the Xibalbans went crazy at the sight." Then Hunahpu is revived. " 'Get up!' he said, and Hunahpu came back to life."

Overwhelmed by these magical powers, the Lords of Death ask the inevitable. "Do it to us! Sacrifice us!" said One and Seven Death. Realizing they have gained the crucial upper hand the Twins sacrifice the Lords but *do not* bring them back to life.

Through trickery the Twins have triumphed in the midst of an extraordinary ordeal through achieving self-knowledge and the powers of self-transformation: "Such was the defeat of the rulers of Xibalba. The boys accomplished it only through wonders, only through self-transformation."

The Twins order the remaining Xibalbans to cease their destructive ways or face the same ultimate death as their lords. Then, in a scene reminiscent of the final passage of Dante's *Inferno,* "the two boys ascended this way, here into the middle of the light and they ascended straight on into the sky, and the sun belongs to one and the moon to the other."[19]

In this way the Twins suffered the tortures of the Underworld but gained the knowledge of self-transformation to overcome the threatened final static condition of death. Instead they learned the secrets of self-sacrifice and regeneration and ascended into the celestial levels to become a permanent pattern of renewal, a mythic model for Maya religion.

This engaging story helps us understand more clearly the meaning of the cosmic scene of Pacal's tomb. His descent is vitally important to record because it marked the beginning of another career, the career of struggling to overcome the Lords of Xibalba with the same cunning, courage, and self-transformation of the Twins. And like them Pacal rose to become, as all Maya kings did, the Sun, rising above the horizon in a regular pattern, passing regularly across the heavens, giving the Maya an experience of regeneration.

The Maya Collapse

In spite of these remarkable strategies to insure the regeneration of their world the Classic Maya civilization collapsed rapidly between 800 and 850 CE. We know that in 790 CE at least nineteen different ceremonial centers erected monuments with the Long Count calendar inscribed on them. But by 889 CE only one ceremonial center in the entire Maya region was using this calendar system. Research at Palenque shows a 90 percent population decline over a two-hundred-year period. Other archaeological evidence makes it clear that the most sophisticated urban culture in Mesoamerican history fell into ruins and the population was decimated or fled the area in a rapid fashion.

Although the causes for this collapse are still mostly unknown, large areas of Maya civilization seem to have undergone a series of internal and external stresses, which combined to bring the ceremonial cities into ruin. It appears that intense trading, ceremonial and military expansion, *and* competition between centers led to a weakening of the interlocking fabric that constituted the Maya world. Population explosions likely put undue stress on the agricultural productivity leading to subsistence emergencies, which the population was unable to stop. Food shortages and weather changes may have led to malnutrition and epidemic diseases, which put increased pressures on ceremonial centers to utilize their religious powers to solve. This led to more intense needs for ceremonial displays and rituals that emphasized the role and power of the elites, who grew further and further away from the confidence of the masses. In order to maintain their own levels of luxury and superiority the elites may have intensified their warfare practices in order to obtain necessary goods and sacrificial victims. This may have led to internal rebellions or at least a loss of faith in the royal families.

One or two of these stresses might be manageable by an elite core of priest-kings; but taken as an interlocking series the stresses may have been too severe and total for the society to survive. In this way the Maya of Palenque, Tikal, Copán, and other magnificent ceremonial centers withered from prominence. It is a pattern we in the modern world must learn about because, like the Maya, our remarkable material achievements may also fade back into the natural landscape.

At any rate the central role of the ceremonial city persisted into the Post-Classic Period and into the memory of the Maya of colonial Guatemala. One passage in the *Popul Vuh,* reads,

"Let us go ourselves and search,
and we shall see for ourselves
whether there is something to guard our sign.
We will find what we should say before them,
and thus we shall live.
There are no guardians for us,"
then said Jaguar Quiche,
Jaguar Night,
Nought, and Wind Jaguar.
They heard news of a city
and went there.[20]

CHAPTER V

Mesoamerica as a New World: Colonialism and Religious Creativity

Although they did not use the term "Latin America," Spaniards and Portuguese thought of America in a unitary way, as a "New World" so different and unknown that it had to be invented, a place where legends about earthly paradises, Amazon women, Prester John, cities of gold and millennial kingdoms might come true. The legends and fantasies of Latin America have continued to be reinvented in the form of romantic stories of island castaways like Robinson Crusoe, and in glossy travel brochures inviting the foreign visitor to unspoiled island paradises and golden lands.

> William B. Taylor[1]

. . . in Mexico City there is never tragedy but only outrage . . . city of the violated outrage, city witness to all we forget, city of fixed sun, city ancient in light, old city cradled among birds of omen, city tempested by domes, city woven by amnesias, bitch city, hungry city, city in the true image of gigantic heaven. Incandescent prickly pear.

> Carlos Fuentes[2]

We have come to the final chapter in our exploration of Meso-american religions and the interrelations between cosmovision and ceremonial centers. Throughout this study we have emphasized that religion is both a matter of the imagination and a matter of the social and material world within which humans dwell. Now we have the task of exploring some of the *continuities and changes* of Mesoamerican religions in the social and symbolic settings that became known as a New World.

In the first chapter we outlined some of the powerful and dehumanizing "inventions" of Mesoamerica and its native peoples. Europeans unleashed both powerful fantasies and colonial expeditions into Mesoamerica, attempting to transform the lands and peoples into extensions of themselves. On the surface Anahuac became Nueva España, the Mexica became Indians, and their religions were considered the devil's work. But beneath the surface indigenous and European traditions mixed together into a remarkable series of new cultural combinations. The food, language, medical practices, even the biological and cultural character of people were transformed into new social and symbolic forms. As Elizabeth Weismann writes in her invaluable *Mexico in Sculpture: 1521–1821,* "Two different kinds of life absorbed each other and produced things new and different from anything else in the world."[3] These new and different things had to be put into new relationships with one another. Most crucial of all, perhaps, were the efforts to locate where the natives and the *mestizos* were to fit in the new social, legal, and religious schemes. The result has been a complex, varied, and sometimes mysterious social and symbolic landscape mixing Aztec, Maya, Otomi, Huichol, Tzutujil, and many other traditions with Catholic, Spanish, Portuguese, French, and other Old World cultural and religious patterns. The student of colonial and modern Mesoamerica is faced with, as the Mexican novelist Carlos Fuentes indicates, a world of outrage, Christian churches, denial of the damage of colonialism, ancient images still visible in daily life, and the persistence of a cosmovision embedded in the largest urban center of the world, Mexico City, "city of the true image of gigantic heaven." Mesoamerica's pre-Columbian traditions have continued to play a vital role in the colonial and postcolonial communities of Mexico, Guatemala, El Salvador, Honduras, Nicaragua, Costa Rica, and Belize. Meaningful traces of these traditions can even be found in the Chicano communities in the United States. And as the Latin American historian William B. Taylor notes above, fantasies about the paradises of Mesoamerica continue to attract people from all over the world.

In this chapter we will look at a series of creative religious responses to the crisis of colonialism that show some of the continuities and changes that have taken place in Mesoamerican religions. We will focus on the human trauma caused by the conquest and early colonial events, and a series of religious practices and responses in contemporary Mesoamerica. These include the peyote hunt of the Huichol Indians, the cult of the **Virgin of Guadalupe,** the **Dia de los Muertos** (Day of the Dead) ceremonies, and the Fiesta de Santiago in Santiago, Atitlan, Guatemala. Each of these ceremonies will be discussed in relation to two major dimensions of religious life in Mesoamerica: pilgrimage and **syncretism.** In each of these traditions people take special journeys to or through a sacred landscape in order to have a direct experience and gain new knowledge of the sacred. These journeys involve, to varying degrees, the three processes we have emphasized in this book: worldmaking, worldcentering, and worldrenewing. The Fiesta of Santiago includes all three dimensions, but emphasizes worldrenewing by symbolically traveling from the *axis mundi* of the community to the four quarters of the universe and back to the center. The Huichol peyote hunt emphasizes worldcentering by traveling to the ancestral lands to gather and consume peyote in order to discover the relationship between humans and ancestral gods and thereby to find the meaning of what it is to be Huichol. And the Dia de los Muertos, practiced in almost every home in Tlaxcala, Mexico, focuses on the family altar, full of foods, gifts, and photographs of the dead, which is an example of worldmaking. But in each case a pilgrimage of humans or spirits is central to the religious action.

A second important dimension of these activities is what scholars call syncretism. Though syncretism can work in a complex fashion involving languages, religions, and other cultural elements, it can be defined simply as "the combination of different forms of beliefs and practices into new patterns of meaning."[4] In religious terms this usually involves the mixing of symbols, ritual elements, or images from different traditions, such as Catholic and Aztec fertility rites, Maya and Catholic devotion to deities, or observances of the dead.

Throughout Mesoamerica today groups carry out ceremonies combining a wide range of native and Catholic symbols and beliefs into new patterns of meanings. And it is primarily within the experience of ritual action that syncretism becomes an authentic dimension of life. For the rituals create the legitimate setting and charged atmosphere for the placing of incongruent objects, symbols, sounds, and ideas together in an acceptable way. This results in new versions of older patterns. The images of Christ and the Saints have received a rich series of innovations in Mexico. A good example are the many colonial churchyard crosses that still stand in Mexico. Many appear, on first glance, to be symbols of a European Christian presence. But on closer view it

This anonymous painting depicts Juan Diego presenting a bouquet of roses and the image of Guadalupe to Bishop Zumárraga, not shown, which according to legend he received from an apparition of the Virgin. Guadalupe spoke to him in Nahuatl from the hilltop previously dedicated to the Aztec goddess Tonantzin. The cult surrounding Our Lady of Guadalupe played a powerful role in integrating colonial society, and the image became a precious symbol of Mexican nationalism. Today, the original image of Guadalupe can be viewed in her Basilica in Mexico City. (Photograph courtesy of the National Catholic News Service.)

is clear that many echo preconquest designs, emotions, conceptions of spatial arrangement, and style. Further reflections leads to the realization that these crosses are neither European nor Indian, but Mexican—a fluid syncretic image of new power, decoration, and combined meanings. Often it is the *mestizo* or Indian community that takes the initiative in forming these meaningful combinations as a means of gaining some measure of power within a cultural situation that has diminished their status or degraded their power. Throughout this chapter we shall see examples of syncretistic combinations and ritual processes in Mesoamerican religions.

The Social and Symbolic Crisis of the Colonial New World

It is also important to recall that this book began with a report of the European invasion and so-called conquest of Mesoamerica. The violent, transformative process of colonialism, which began in the

1520s in Mexico, Guatemala, and other regions of Mesoamerica, radically altered (to varying degrees) the social and symbolic worlds of the Moctezumas, Quetzalcoatls, Hero Twins, *calpullis, altepetls,* ceremonial centers, and communities at large. This process has been consistently referred to as having created a "New World" with its smaller "New Spain," and then eventually "New Mexico" and along the north Atlantic coast "New York," "New England," "New Jersey," "Nova Scotia," and so forth. However, the natives of Mesoamerica who underwent the process of colonialism experienced this newness more as forms of dependency, oppression, starvation, disease, death, and dehumanization than as opportunities for salvation and revitalization. It was a "newness" they could have just as well done without. The formation of new religious movements and cults and mixtures of pre-Hispanic and Catholic religious meanings emerged as strategies to survive and maintain human integrity in relation to their lands and selves.

Although we cannot go into an extensive description of the social and biological disasters of the Spanish conquest of Mesoamerica, it is important to state directly how the human population suffered. And it is vital to remember that the colonial process in Mesoamerica began almost one hundred years before the English explored the North American coast and established their settlements at Plymouth and Massachusetts Bay. By the early 1600s, when parts of northern Europe were abuzz with rumors, stories, and prejudices about the people and lands in the New World (these stories and prejudices had largely filtered up from Spain and Portugal), most of the great ceremonial centers and local shrines in the Aztec, Tlaxcalan, Tarascan, and other kingdoms had been dismantled and replaced by Christian churches well under construction. American history does not begin in New England, as is still taught in public schools in the United States. It started in Yucatan, Tlaxcala, Cholula, Tenochtitlan, and it was characterized by misunderstanding, greed, warfare, theft, disease, debate, economic exchange, and a ferocious clash of two types of cosmovisions.

The conquest and colonial process in Mesoamerica had a devastating impact on the human population. The tie between the colonizer and the colonized was often violent and authoritarian. But what really devastated the indigenous population was disease. Although it is not easy to determine the quantative loss of life, historians have been able to estimate with reliable plausibility that in 1500 around 80 million inhabitants occupied the New World. By 1550 only 10 million natives were alive. In Mexico there were close to 25 million people in 1500. By 1600 only 1 million native Mesoamericans were still alive. This incredible loss of life was caused by either direct murder in warfare, cruelty in the mines, fields, and towns, or "microbe shock," that is, diseases. The majority of the indigenous population who died during the sixteenth century were the victims of diseases transmitted by the "lethal handshake"—the physical contact with Europeans including baptism by Catholic priests. These diseases turned into epidemics fueled by malnutrition, fatigue, and the destruction of the indigenous social relations and medical practices. People in Mesoamerica had had their own diseases and epidemics, which periodically caused crisis prior to the European colonies. But the immune systems developed in the pre-Columbian periods were not prepared to face the diseases transmitted by Europeans and the result was catastrophic.

When surveying the destructive consequences of European presence in Mesoamerica, it is important to also state that many Europeans cared deeply for the native people and made serious and sustained efforts to understand the native culture and to work out ways of fitting them into the new society. It is also very important to realize that the natives responded in varying degrees to the problems and challenges of the new society. Some fell into complete despair, whereas others strove with varying degrees of success to find places in society that combined indigenous and foreign elements into their lives. During the sixteenth and seventeenth centuries a new society and culture, unique in the history of humankind, took form and expression in Mesoamerica.

We can see both the pressures to change indigenous society and the attempt by natives to find a place in the strange, new world created by the conquest in this passage from the *Book of Chilam Balam of Tizimin* (p. 45).

> Your older brothers are arriving
> To change your pants,
> To change your clothes,
> To whiten your dress,
> To whiten your pants—

The foreign judges,
The bearded men
Of heaven born Merida,
The seat of the lands.
And they
Are the sun priests
Of the living God,
The true God.
He shall be worshiped
In one communion
On earth
Below:
An additional rule.
And for the fatherless,
And for the motherless—
Jaguar was the head
And urged his people
To be sprinkled
In the changed city.

The passage tells how the Maya were told that the Spaniards were coming to change society, customs, and religion. The Maya will be forced to change their clothes, new judges will issue laws from Merida, the capital, and the religion of what the missionaries said was the true God was being introduced. Finally, the Maya leader, the "Jaguar" in the text, urges the people to become converted to Catholicism, "to be sprinkled in the changed city," that is, the colonial city of Merida.

But in the early part of the colonial process the Indian population was in grave crisis. The gravity of the colonial situation is reflected in the writings of the Franciscan priest Motolinia, who compared the devastation of the indigenous populations with the ten plagues sent by God to chastise the Egyptians in the Old Testament. The first plague was smallpox: "They died in heaps, like bedbugs." The second plague was the death by Spanish weapons. The third was the famine that accompanied the Spanish destruction of Indian harvests. The fourth plague was the vicious overseers who tortured the natives. The fifth plague was the taxes in the forms of lands and goods levied on the natives. The Indians were under such pressure that when they had no goods they were forced to sell their children to the Spaniards, and eventually to sell themselves. The sixth plague were the mines in which Indians were forced to work long hours in dangerous conditions and sometimes carry loads as heavy as 250 pounds up steep underground ascents. The seventh plague was the building of the city of Mexico, during which scores of Indians died in falls, were crushed by beams, or were crushed by buildings being torn down. The eighth plague was the slavery of the mines. Slaves were branded by the letters of all those who bought and sold them. In some cases a slave was tattooed with brands on many parts of his or her body. The ninth plague was the open graveyards around the mines. One eyewitness wrote,

> For half a league around these mines and along a great part of the road one could scarcely avoid walking over dead bodies or bones, and the flocks of birds and crows that came to feed upon the corpses were so numerous that they darkened the sun . . .[5]

The tenth plague was the in-fighting, factions, and scapegoating among the Spaniards. Their internal social problems often led to frustrated excuses for executing large numbers of Indians without legal or rational justification. Consider, for instance, this unbelievable report by the priest Bartolome de las Casas. One day, after a picnic, a group of Spaniards decided to test whether their swords were sharp.

> A Spaniard, in whom the devil is thought to have clothed himself, suddenly drew his sword. Then the whole hundred drew theirs and began to rip open the bellies, to cut and kill those lambs—men, women, children, and old folk all of whom were seated, off guard and frightened, watching the mares and the Spaniards. And within two credos, not a man of all of them there remains alive. The Spaniards enter the large house nearby, for this was happening at its door, and in the same way, with cuts and stabs, begin to kill as many as they found there, so that a stream of blood was running, as if a great number of cows had perished.[6]

It is important to reiterate that there was another community of Spaniards, usually led by priests and nuns, who not only strove to understand the nature of Indian societies but also struggled, sometimes at serious personal risk to stop the abuse, killing, and exploitation of native peoples.

The near extermination of the indigenous population began to be reversed in the eighteenth century. By 1800, as astonishing as it

may seem, there were 6 million Indians living, struggling, and in
isolated cases thinking rebellion, which occasionally broke out, in
different parts of Mesoamerica. There were also a growing number
of *castas* or *mestizos* or people of mixed blood who had more
rights and privileges than the native communities.

The point is that Mesoamerica, in fact all of Latin America, became an incredibly complex world. This complexity has been outlined by William Taylor in his writing on Latin American social
history. Taylor notes that on the one hand there are a number of
common features in the colonial history of the New World, such as

> degradation of the labor force, rural estates, village communities
> (many of which were "peasant" communities in the anthropologists'
> specialized meaning) Independence Wars, urbanizations, and large-
> scale collective actions . . . a conflict society . . . the Spanish Con-
> quest, the Comunero Rebellions, the Tupac Amaru Rebellion, slave
> revolts, the Independence Wars, wars of reform, United States inter-
> ventions, millenarian movements, and social and socialist
> revolutions.[7]

But scholars have also become impressed with the local variations of social developments and religious responses to the order
of the world in the New World. As Taylor notes,

> Recent scholarship describes a notable fluidity of communities—
> much leaving and returning, some movement across lines of rank,
> ethnicity, and class, and vague and permeable boundaries—and sig-
> nificant regional variation in structural changes and institutions . . .[8]

One way of talking about these significant fluidities in terms of religious response is through the category of syncretism, or the process of mixing together elements from different religious traditions.
Syncretism is a sign of important religious change taking place in a
culture, and the primary instrument of that change appears to be
ritual and ceremonial life. Throughout Mesoamerica today indigenous and *mestizo* groups carry out ceremonies combining native
and Catholic symbols and beliefs all the time. One of the most
powerful Christian images that has been joined to indigenous religious ideas is the image of Jesus Christ as suffering savior. The
bleeding, pained image of Jesus on the Cross has had special at-
traction to all social groups and classes in Latin America including
native communities, who see a version of their own sacred tradi-

tions in stories of Christ's passion. A special example of syncretism that joins the image of the crucified Christ to native religion appears in the following tale from Zinacantan, a highland Maya community in Chiapas, Mexico. In it we see an example of religious change at the level of story and myth.

When Christ Was Crucified

When the world was made long ago, the Holy father walked. He made the rocks and sea, corn and trees, everything there is on earth.

When he was chased by the devils he ran. But the devils were right behind him. They saw that there were trees already, peach trees, white sapotes, everything.

"Hurry up, you bastards, he's here now, he's near now.

He's planted everything already."

Our Lord ran around the world. Ooh, he was tired out.

He hid under some banana trees to rest.

"He's near now" said the devils.

The Magpie-jay was there. He was a human then.

"Is it Our Lord you're looking for?" asked the jay.

"He's here now. Seize him!"

They captured Our Lord. They made him carry a cross.

Our Lord bent low to the ground.

They hung him on the cross. He cried. He bled.

"Let's eat! He's dead now," said the devils.

Our Lord was left hanging.

A rooster landed on the arm of the cross.

"Tell me if they are coming," said Our Lord.

"I'll climb back up the cross right away.

"I have more work to do. You call out!"

"All right," said the rooster. "Cock-a doodle-doo!"

Quickly Our Lord climbed up the cross.

"Where are the devils?" he asked.

"Nowhere, they aren't coming," said the rooster.

"What are you good for?" said the Lord.

"This is what you're good for!"

He wrung the rooster's neck until it was dead.

A sparrow appeared.

"You sing out," said our Lord.

"I'm going to work a little while."

The Lord came down from the cross. He looked for a blue pebble.

He threw it into the air. The sky was made.

The sparrow called out. Our Lord climbed up the cross.
All the devils arrived.
"He's still hanging here," they said.
"We killed him. Let's bury him."
He died. He was buried.
"We'll come back three days from now," said the devils.
"They thought I died," said the Lord.
"But I'll revive in three days."
Living he rose to heaven. He left a substitute here on earth.
"The rooster is no good. He can be sacrificed.
"The sparrow mustn't be harmed," said Our Lord.
So, living, he rose to heaven.
He arrived at the right hand of the judge.[9]

This story cannot be fully interpreted here, but syncretism is richly illustrated in this combination of both an indigenous myth about the creation of the cosmos and the story of Jesus's career, crucifixion, and resurrection. In Zinacantec mythology, predating the imposition of Catholicism, the world was made in three stages. In the beginning the rocks and ground were made, then the ocean, trees, and animals appeared. Finally the sky was created. Part of the indigenous creation story appears here with Christ coming down from the cross and throwing a blue pebble into the air to complete the third stage of the creation of the cosmos. "He threw it into the air. The sky was made." Catholic influences mixed with local cosmology appear when the tale tells of Christ rising into heaven to sit at the right hand of the judge. The judge is the Christian saint San Salvador, who occupies the center of the sky. According to the storyteller, Romin Teratol, San Salvador is the older brother of the sun or Christ who was sent to travel around the world to record and report back on the sins of humans.

It is clear that the Zinacantecs know and have incorporated bits of the gospel stories into their creation stories. We see Christ's temptation by the devil, the betrayal by Judas (here in the form of the magpie), his crucifixion, and conversations with the other two crucified victims on Golgotha, and his resurrection included in their version. The story also provides the indigenous ritual prescription that roosters can be used as sacrificial birds in curing ceremonies, house dedications, and agricultural rites. In ceremonies focusing on the treatment of illnesses these birds become the "substitute" of a patient. On the other hand the story is telling that the rufous-collared sparrow cannot be killed by the community because "Our Lord," who is at once Christ and a pre-Columbian deity, blessed the bird.

Syncretism is a rich and varied process of combining religious elements from different traditions; but it is important to emphasize the creativity involved in forming new religious and social combinations, especially in colonial settings like Mesoamerica between 1520 and 1900. One of the most vivid, moving, and beautiful examples of creative syncretism is the pervasive cult of the Virgin of Guadalupe in Mexico, which began within two decades after the conquest and continues to thrive to this day.

The Virgin of Guadalupe

The Virgin of Guadalupe is part of a much larger cult of the Virgin Mary of Immaculate Conception, which permeates religious art, meaning, and practice throughout Latin America. Images of the different sacred Virgins are found on statues, clothes, and jewelry in every conceivable place in Latin countries, including churches, bars, discotheques, restaurants, ballfields, hotels, museums, chapels, ice cream shops, parks, and automobiles.

From 1540 to today the cult of Mary has dominated churches and even entire villages, which turn to her as the go-between to God the Father and believe that the destiny of the whole community depends on her powers. Powerful cults dedicated to Mary include the cult of the Virgin of los Remedios, the Virgin of Candelaria at San Juan de los Lagos, and the Virgin of Zapopan. It is obvious that the Virgin Mary is a European importation into Mesoamerica. Each Iberian colonial incursion into Mesoamerica was accompanied, if not led, by the standard of one of the Virgins, who protected, inspired, and comforted the invaders as they claimed new territories and peoples for the Spanish empire. But in each case new meanings were given to the Spanish cult of the Virgin by *mestizos,* Indians, and creoles (Spaniards born in the New World). This remarkable creativity shows in clearer outline what we saw suggested in the Zinacantec story of Jesus, namely, that the native peoples and *mestizos* did, in varying degrees, embrace elements of Christianity, came to regard themselves as Christians, and developed new forms of Christian stories, art, and ritual expression. But this process of becoming and transforming Christian meanings and practices was wonderfully complex and difficult to describe adequately.

The cult of the Virgin of Guadalupe contains many of the rich patterns of religious life we have studied in this book, including pilgrimage, *axis mundi,* worldrenewal, ecstasy, and syncretism. According to the official tradition in Mexico a dark-skinned Virgin of Guadalupe appeared to a lowly Indian who was passing by the hill of Tepeyac in 1531, just ten years after the capital of Tenochtitlan fell to Cortés's forces. When the Indian, Juan Diego, reported the apparition to church authorities, they immediately scoffed at the idea that the Mother of Jesus would reveal herself to an Indian. When Juan Diego returned to the site to ask for the apparition's assistance she told him in Nahuatl to take roses from a nearby bush that was blooming out of season and roll them up in his cloak. He did as he was told, and when he unrolled the cloak a magnificent color image of the Virgin of Guadalupe, surrounded by a blazing solar corona, was imprinted on it. When Juan Diego took the cloak to the Archbishop of Mexico, according to popular legend, the astonishing miracle was accepted and the site of the revelation was chosen for the future cathedral. Today Mexico's greatest basilica stands at the bottom of the hill and is visited every day by thousands of the faithful, who gaze upward at the glass-encased cloak with the miraculously painted image of the Virgin. Some come in pilgrimages from hundreds of miles away and walk the last part on their knees, praying along the way.

Even in the middle of the sixteenth century, priests complained that there were "idols behind altars" (pre-Columbian pagan statues, or memories of statues, behind the Catholic altars) at places like Tepeyac. On the one hand, however, the apparition of Guadalupe was familiar and even affirmed by the Spaniards who brought a tradition of apparitions and shrines to the New World. Mexico was a training ground for priests who expected apparitions to be part of their ministry. On the other hand the Franciscans and Dominican priests, who spoke Nahuatl and observed the indigenous peoples adjusting painfully to the colonial order, realized that the Indians were not merely adopting Spanish Catholic practices. Rather they were mixing native and European beliefs together and sometimes disguising their continued worship of their spirits, deities, and ancestors in their devotion to Mary and other saints. It was known that the site of Juan Diego's experience was the sacred hill dedicated to the Aztec mother goddess, Tonantzin, who was worshiped throughout the history of the Aztec empire. Recently archaeoastronomers and historians of religions have shown how Tepeyac was associated with important pre-Columbian ceremonial routes traveled to stimulate the rain-giving mountains to release their vital waters. It appears that Aztec ceremonial life involved ceremonial pilgrimages and processions to many of the sacred mountains around the Valley of Mexico and that Tepeyac and its nearby hills were shrines of high importance to the rain god cults of Tenochtitlan. The point is that the cult of Guadalupe, while strongly Catholic in meaning, also expresses an Indian sense of sacred space and worship of a goddess and her cults.

One of the most difficult realizations for students of religion to reach is the multiple, sometimes contradictory meanings of symbols or religious images. In a religious cosmovision, whether in Mesoamerica or Europe or China, a single symbol will have multiple meanings. An obvious example of this multivalence is the Christian cross. On the one hand it represents the betrayal, suffering, sacrifice, and death of Jesus Christ. But on the other hand it represents resurrection, life, victory over death, and faith in God. This multiplicity of meanings is also stimulated by the local variations a symbol or deity may take according to local history, geography, politics, and ecology. There are many local meanings and stories associated with the different holy virgins in Mexico. At the same time Guadalupe is special because she integrates the tensions of Indians and Spaniard, *mestizo* and Indian, Spaniard and *mestizo* into *one* community of faith and devotion.

We can see very different images and meanings associated with Guadalupe during her career in Mexico. First, she is considered the nurturing Mother who embraces, protects, and loves the people and nation of Mexico. She is kind, loving, forgiving, and accessible in all the shrines and images dedicated to her. Second, she is the wonderful intercessor, the go-between to whom humans turn in order to reach the miraculous power of God the Father. Third, she can also become the female warrior of the revolution. At different, violent upheavals in Mexican history priests and rebels have turned to her power and authority to inspire them to overthrow the oppressive government. She becomes the natural ally of the common people, often Indians and *mestizos,* in their spirit of rebellion. She is approached for aid in the resistance against hated taxes. For example, in the Indian uprising in Tulancingo in 1769, rebel leaders called for the death of Spanish officials and the creation of an Indian priesthood.

> They dreamed of the day when bishops and the alcaldes mayores would kneel and kiss the rings of the native priests. Their new theocratic utopia was led by an Indian who called himself the New Savior and by a consort who was reputed to be the Virgin of Guadalupe.[10]

In Guadalupe we see a curious and even furious syncretistic mixture. She is Indian and Spaniard. She is an Earth Mother and a Holy Mother. She is a comforter and a revolutionary. She is the magnet for pilgrimages and she is a pilgrim herself, traveling in front of the rebel soldiers and entering every heart who needs her protection and comfort, as did the poor Indian Juan Diego in 1531.

The Peyote Hunt of the Huichol Indians

Not all religious practices in contemporary Mesoamerica have a mixture of indigenous and imported symbols and beliefs. In some cases Nahuatl and Maya-speaking peoples practice pre-Columbian rituals that have very little Catholic or Protestant influence. One outstanding example, witnessed by cultural anthropologist Barbara Myerhoff, is the yearly Huichol pilgrimage to **Wirikuta,** the land of the ancestors where *hikuri,* or peyote, grows.

The Huichol peoples live in the mountainous regions of the Mexican states of Durango, Jalisco, Nayarit, and Zacatecas. The Huichols are famous for their brilliantly colored yarn paintings, which depict myths, images, and fantastic beings from their worldview and environment. Their social and symbolic life is complex and varied, but they are best known for their yearly journey to the ancestral territory of Wirikuta, 200 miles from the city of Guadalajara, in search of peyote and peyote visions. These pilgrimages are always led by a shaman-priest or **mara 'akame** such as Ramon Medina Silva, who was the chief informant in Barbara Myerhoff's study *Peyote Hunt: The Sacred Journey of the Huichol Indians.*

Ramon's role and original decision to become a **mara 'akame** represents our earlier discussion about the human career as a way of worldcentering. When he was between six and nine years old Ramon began to have a series of amazing dreams in which the Huichol deity Tayaupa (Our Father Sun) spoke to him, revealing that he was being chosen to become a spiritual leader of the Huichols.

> Tayaupa spoke to me. He said, "Look, son, do not worry. You must grow a little more so you can go out and become wise, so that you can support yourself . . . You will make fine things, things of color. You will understand this and that. It is for this that you were born." At first, I was frightened. I did not know. I began to reflect.[11]

During this period of reflection Ramon was bitten by a snake and nearly died. His grandfather, a **mara 'akame,** healed him and it was slowly revealed to the community that Ramon had been chosen by the Huichol gods to become a shaman-priest. This combination of religious dreams and injury/healing is typical of individuals who become set apart from the community into a status of sacred leader.

Years later Barbara Myerhoff was introduced to the adult artist/shaman Ramon Medina and became a trusted friend of his family. After two summers of visits, conversations, and taped question-and-answer sessions Myerhoff was invited to participate, under Ramon's guidance, in the sacred journey to Wirikuta.

The peyote hunt, which is described in some detail by Myerhoff, and which appears in Peter Furst's film *To Find Our Life,* has many stages and powerful transitions in it. According to Myerhoff the journey to Wirikuta, 200 miles to the north, is the Huichol version of a universal human quest, namely the search for Paradise, or the original center of the world where god, human, animal, and plant were at one with each other during a primordial era. This search for a total unity or *communitas* with all of life is reflected in two major themes of the peyote hunt. First, the pilgrims are changed, through a ritual, into living images of the first peyote pilgrims, who were gods. The pilgrims are gods in human form. Second, the peyote plant is also identified with the deer (animal ances-tor). In the Huichol past the deer was a source of food and beauty, a magical animal who is remembered as having given the first peyote to the first peyote hunters. On each subsequent hunt it is believed that the peyote is left by the ancestral deer who comes from the sky. Only the *mara 'akame* can see him, while the other pilgrims can see his footprints in the forms of peyote plants in the desert floor. This unity of animal and plant is further enriched by the symbolism of the maize in Huichol thought. Maize is the source of life today, abundant and all around. In the Huichol cos-movision the peyote hunt is a time and action of unity bringing together animal and plant, past and present, ancestor, spirit, and the human. Therefore the peyote hunt must be carried out with the utmost care.

This experience of unity is achieved through a series of stages that make up the drama of the hunt. The Huichols sing, dance, play music, and chant during the peyote hunt, which can be said to have the following stages: Stage one is preparation and rehears-al, stage two is taking the names of deities, and stage three is pre-paring the fire and confessions. These first three stages take place at a private home before stage four, departure for Wirikuta, which is about a twenty-day walk from Huichol communities. Today they drive in cars and trucks. Arrival at Tatei Matinieri (Where Our Mother Dwells), a place of natural springs in the desert, is stage five. There the pilgrims witness the sunrise and "help Tayaupa come up."

At each stage there are meaningful and emotional moments of sadness, joy, exuberance, and solemnity, according to the occasion. In stage six reversals are established in which the people, now con-sidered living images of the first peyote pilgrims, are designated as the opposite of what they in fact are. For instance,

> Merriment and excitement filled the car and animated chatter and laughter. By way of explaining the laughter, Ramon reached over and taking some of my hair in his hand said that now it was cactus fiber. Pointing to himself, he said that he was the Pope, that Lupe (his pretty wife) was an "ugly boy," Victoria a gringa, and Francisco (the oldest male) a nunutsi (little child).[12]

The meaning of these reversals is that the *peyoteros* are partici-pating in *another mode of being,* a religious way of being human, and as such change or reverse who they are. This is partly due to the fact that each peyote hunt repeats the first peyote hunt, when the ancestral gods journeyed to Wirikuta.

The seventh stage is the arrival at Wirikuta, which is signified by the "knotting-in," an act of unification of the pilgrims when they tie knots in a string that links them together at the entrance to the sacred land. Stage eight includes the actual "hunt" of peyote, which is considered in Huichol symbolism to be a deer. Myerhoff's description helps us understand this identification of plant and animal.

> The hikuritamete (peyote companions) set out across the desert, moving briskly toward the mountains but fanning out instead of following the single file usually observed for ritual processions. Everyone was completely quiet and grave, looking closely at the ground for tracks. As they approached the mountains, the peyoteros' pace slackened for peyote was more likely to be found here and the tension mounted. Their behavior was precisely that of stalking an animal. There were no sudden movements, no talking. The pilgrims bent over close to the ground, moved in the brush on tiptoe, gingerly raising a branch or poking under a cactus in hopes of catching sight of the small gray-green peyote plant which is so inconspicuous, growing nearly parallel to the earth's surface and exactly the same color as surrounding vegetation in this region. . . . Finally Ramon beckoned everyone to his side—he had found peyote, seen the deer. Quickly we all gathered behind him as he drew his arrow and readied the bow. We peered down at the barely noticeable round flat-topped plant, two inches in diameter, segregated into eight sections. Everyone prayed quietly as Ramon began to stalk it, moving ever closer until when he was only a few feet away he aimed and shot one arrow into the base of the plant toward the east and crossed it quickly with another arrow pointing north so that the peyote was impaled in the center. The peyote-deer was thus secured and unable to escape.[13]

Following a series of prescribed ritual actions the *peyoteros* collect, sort, clean, and pack a large number of peyote buttons. During several following nights peyote is eaten by the group gathered around the fire in order to induce visions. The pilgrims laugh and discuss the beautiful colors and little animals in their visions, finally falling quiet as they stare into the fire. During this entire episode the **mara 'akame** gazes quietly into the fire seeing visions of the ancestral pilgrims, the spirits of the Huichol cosmos. He sees and talks with the main deities, receiving new knowledge about life and the sacred.

Stage nine is the departure from Wirikuta. This involves the giving of peyote names, the eating of salt, and the untying of the cord that united the group before entering the sacred land.

In this remarkable sacred journey, the Huichol regenerate their sense of identity. In their words, they "find our life," meaning they commune with the beauty and powers of Wirikuta and come to experience what it feels like and what one "sees" when one is a Huichol. All this is a reiteration of how the world of the peyote hunt was first made.

Having looked at a pilgrimage in which people travel to a sacred space to find their life, let us now turn to the yearly celebrations called Day of the Dead, in which the spirits of deceased friends and relatives make the pilgrimage back into the world of the living.

Dia de los Muertos (Day of the Dead)

One of the most meaningful yearly celebrations in Mexico, in fact throughout Latin America, is the Dia de los Muertos (Day of the Dead) celebrated for nearly a week at the end of October and beginning of November. This elaborate celebration, dedicated to the cult of the dead (also referred to as Todos Santos, All Saints Day), combines pre-Hispanic rituals and beliefs with Catholic practices and symbols. The central idea is that during this period of public and private (family) rituals the living and dead family members and friends are joined together in an atmosphere of communion and spiritual regeneration.

It is important to note that the rituals, symbols, and elaborate decorations of home altars and cemeteries are somewhat different according to region. Some communities will emphasize elaborate cemetery altars and decorations, while others will emphasize the processions between home and cemetery. Still others make unusual efforts to decorate their home altars to dead ancestors in baroque, lavish ways. Some communities have open-air competitions of altars and offerings to the dead, ranging from small altars to some that are 10 feet high and 50 feet long. But all Day of the Dead celebrations focus on a spiritual covenant between the human community and supernatural entities of deceased family members, friends, or saints. The following description is taken largely from Day of the Dead celebrations in the Mexican state of Tlaxcala, east of Mexico City, as reported by Hugo Nutini.

The Day of the Dead rituals are complex and difficult to categorize, but we can emphasize three outstanding dimensions: the preparations for the ceremonies (worldmaking), the symbolism of the family altars to the dead (worldcentering), and the ceremonial feast of the dead, and spiritual union with the dead at the home and cemetery (worldrenewal).

Scholars have determined that important elements of the Day of the Dead festivities were practiced in pre-Hispanic times and have become integrated into the Catholic traditions of Latin America. Bernardino de Sahagun discovered the following ritual practices associated with the month of Tepeilhuitl in the Aztec capital. In this description we see the importance of the cult of the dead associated with a ceremonial place.

> They also used to place the image of the dead on those grass wreaths. Then at dawn they put these images in their shrines, on top of beds of reed mace, sedge, or rush. Once the images were placed there, they offered them food, tamales, and gruel, or a stew made of chicken (turkey) or dog's meat. Then they offered the images incense from an incense burner, which was a big cup full of coals, and this ceremony they called calonoac.
>
> And the rich sang and drank pulcre (fermented agave juice) in honor of these gods and their dead, while the poor offered them only food, as has been mentioned.[14]

This same pattern of offering food to the spirits of dead ancestors in ceremonial shrines is carried out today after elaborate and sometimes economically stressful preparations.

In each household, which is the center of the cult of the dead, it is believed that the souls of the dead have taken a journey to the world beyond. The souls of good people travel a straight and narrow path to another world, while the souls of bad people travel a wide and labyrinthine way. All souls arrive at a deep and broad river that can only be crossed with the help of a dog, which lifts the souls on his shoulders and carries them over to the other side.

In Tlaxcala, at least, it is believed that the bad souls would be refused transportation across this river, while good souls could persuade the dog to carry them more easily if they had coins that were placed in the mouth or hand of the dead at their funerals. In many communities it is believed that dogs must be treated well in this life because they are spirit helpers in the next.

What is outstanding in all cases is the belief that one's life on this earth is dependent, in part, on treating the dead well. People believe that if the dead are not worshiped, nurtured, and remembered in the proper manner their own economic security, family stability, and health will be in jeopardy. Therefore careful and generous preparations are carried out.

Preparations (Worldmaking)

Prominent in the decorations of family altars and cemetery altars are the marigold flowers or *zempoalxochitl* (a Nahuatl word meaning "20-flower"). Most households grow their own *zempoalxochitl* in their own gardens and plant the seeds in the middle of August so that the flowers bloom by the last part of October. This sense of preparation for Dia de los Muertos intensifies at the start of October, when people set out the necessary cash and other goods to be used in the generous decorations of altars, tombs, and at the ceremonial meals for the dead and the living. Also, careful arrangements are made to be free from jobs so that the proper ritual responsibilities can be carried out. In Latin America, where poverty is so widespread, this responsibility entails a sense of sacrifice on behalf of the family. Journeys are made to local and regional markets, sometimes covering several hundred miles, so that the correct foods and decorations can be purchased in time for the sacred week.

Most important are preparations of special foods for the dead. These include baked breads, candied fruit, skulls made of sugar, and human figurines made of pumpkin seeds, as well as apple, pear, and quince preserves. Papier-mâché images of various kinds are purchased or made, to be used in the decorations of the altars and the cemetery graves. The last and most crucial item to be picked or purchased are the *zempoalxochitl* flowers. Since these flowers will last for only four days, they are placed on altars and tombs, and as pathways between the cemeteries and the homes on the day before Dia de los Muertos begins.

The Family Altar (Worldcentering)

Day of the Dead altars can appear in public plazas, in schools, and even in competitions, but the most important altar appears in the individual household. Within the family home it serves as the *axis mundi* of the ritual and ceremonial life of the family. Most homes in the Tlaxcala region will have an altar in place all year round, but it becomes elaborately and colorfully decorated during this ritual period. This altar becomes a sacred precinct or, in the words of the subtitle of this book, a ceremonial center within the home made up of at least ten kinds of objects—breads, sweets, cooked dishes, delicacies, fruits and vegetables, liquors and liquids, flowers and plants, clothing, adornments, and (perhaps most important) pictures, images, and statues. These pictures and statues are usually placed in a *retablo* (a structure forming the back of an altar), where images of the Virgin, Christ, the cross, and saints watch over the *ofrenda,* or offering to the dead. This offering takes the shape of a wonderful feast for the spirits of the dead who will return and be nourished on specific nights during Dia de los Muertos. A typical *ofrenda* in Tlaxcala is shaped like a four-sided pyramid decorated along the edges by *zempoalxochitl* flowers. At each of the four corners are placed mounds of mandarins and oranges on top of sugar cane cuttings. Cooked dishes, liquids, finger foods, *pan de muerto* loaves, candied fruits, tamales, bananas, and oranges constitute the bulk of the offering. The most impressive objects of the *ofrenda* are crystallized sugar skulls of different sizes and with various kinds of decorations. These skulls represent the dead infants, children, and adults being honored that year.

Many rich symbolic and social meanings are expressed in this crowded, organic ceremonial center. This cornucopia of goods represents the quest for fertility and the renewal of relations with dead friends and family members. But the overall image is that of a sacred Mountain of Sustenance that orients and nourishes the family community. As we have seen in our chapter on the Aztec ceremonial pyramids the Mountain of Sustenance is a pre-Catholic symbol of rain, fertility, and the container of the most valued supernatural powers. In part the Dia de Los Muertos altars and *ofrendas* symbolize the body of the life-giving earth with its forces of regeneration.

Communion with the Dead (Worldrenewing)

The actual moments of reunion with the dead and the regeneration of family ties are carefully orchestrated. In fact, according to the detailed practices of the Tlaxcala region, there are five categories of the dead souls who return on five consecutive days: those who die in accidents, those who die violently, those who die as infants, dead children, and dead adults. On November 2, which is the climax of Todos Santos, all the dead are remembered.

According to Hugo Nutini's research in Tlaxcala the people believe that the souls of the dead begin to return and hover around their family households beginning at 3 PM on October 31. In order for the souls of the dead to return to the house where they lived, a trail of *zempoalxochitl* flowers must be laid out for them to find their way. Early in the morning the women in the family prepare a basket of fragrant flower petals, which are sprinkled with holy water from the church. Then the male adults and children lay the petals in a line marking a trail from the street through the yard or courtyard to the foot of the family altar. This trail is intended to show the spirits of the dead the path home from the cemetery. It is important that the flowers be fragrant because it is believed that while the souls of the dead are blind, they have acute senses of smell and can find their way home on the path of aroma created by the petals.

By 9 PM on November 1 it is believed that all the souls of the dead have traveled along the fragrant path of flowers to their old homes. In some homes the room containing the altar/*ofrenda* is closed between 10 PM and 6 AM so that the returning souls can enjoy the food and treats and reminisce together about their past lives in the human world. Then it is believed that the souls of the dead return to the cemetery to join the living in a vigil of communion.

This vigil is called Xochatl in Nahuatl or La Llorada in Spanish (the Weeping), and it is the time when the living and dead join together as a living spiritual community. The souls of the dead reassure the living of their continued protection, and the living reassure the dead that they will remember and nurture them in their daily lives.

In the local cemetery a community band with *teponaxtle y chirimia* (native drum and flute) ensemble play both melancholy and vibrant tunes for eight hours while candles are lit on the graves and rosaries are said as church bells toll out pleasing music for the souls of the dead who are about to return to their graves. The living ask the dead souls to protect their families, crops, businesses, health, and property for another year. Part of the ritual speech goes, "Oh, blessed souls who have kindly returned to us . . . to participate with us in this day of remembrance, find it in the goodness of your hearts to protect us and shelter us.[15]

Here we see a moving example of modern-day Mesoamericans, heirs of centuries of both a pre-Hispanic cosmovision and Catholic patterns of rosaries and altars, regenerating their own sense of family and community by participating in the cult of the dead.

The Fiesta of Santiago Among the Tzutujil Maya

Earlier we studied the symbolism of the cosmic tree and the rituals of bleeding for a vision of regeneration among the Classic Maya (third to ninth centuries CE). We also traveled through the underworld with the Maya Hero Twins of the seventeenth-century document *Popul Vuh*. Now we will turn to the festival of Santiago, held the third week in July in the Guatemalan Maya community of Santiago Atitlan. In spite of the harsh history the Maya have undergone since the first half of the sixteenth century, the contemporary Maya of Santiago Atitlan (known regionally as Atitecos) have devised effective strategies to maintain many of their traditional ways of worldrenewing by mixing them with Catholic practices and holidays. Agricultural fertility and renewal was an essential dimension of all Maya communities. Consider the contemporary ritual methods for insuring worldrenewal during the Feast of Santiago or, as the Maya call it, *nim q'ij Santiag* or Big Sun Santiago.

This ceremony takes place when the first corn is being harvested in the highland Maya region, around July 23, which is also the saint's day of Santiago (Saint James) in the Catholic calendar.

Throughout contemporary Mesoamerica Santiago has a rich range of meanings in the many local societies where he is represented in rite, iconography, and theology. To the Atitecos, Santiago is identified as a Catholic saint and also as a *bokunab,* a category of deity characterized by the power to multiply elements of the world they come in contact with. Although this characteristic is most notable for its relationship to agricultural abundance, with Santiago it is portrayed symbolically by his sword. When Santiago whacks people with a sword it doesn't kill, but instead divides his target into two. If he touches corn it increases in number. In other words *bokunabs* not only regenerate the world, they make it more abundant. This idea is combined in Maya religion with the belief that humans have a responsibility for assisting in this process of enrichment by carrying out certain rituals in a correct manner. This is a way of taking care of the divine forces so they will continue to regenerate the cosmos.

The following description of the ritual celebration of Santiago comes from interviews with Robert Carlsen, a cultural anthropologist who has lived among the Tzutujil Maya for parts of ten years during which he witnessed and participated in the *nim q'ij.* His experience has been significantly enriched by a personal, working relationship with Martin Prechtel, a shaman healer (*a'kun*) who was initiated by Nicolas Chiveleyo, a renowned Maya leader, into Maya ritual traditions. Speaking of the almost twelve-hour ritual procession, which symbolically travels to the four quarters of the Atiteco universe, Carlsen stated,

> The celebration begins early in the morning when members of the town's ten different *cofradias* (traditional religious organizations) gather at the cathedral in their colorful, woven costumes. Several of the *cofradias* bring the statue of a saint, each lavishly dressed and mounted on a platform which is carried on the shoulders of members of the *cofradia.* These saints have been in the church for several days, waiting for the long, slow walk around the block, which is also the Tzutujil cosmos in miniature. In the minds of the Atitecos, these statues are living images of the deities, which combine Christian and Maya attributes, and these living images are pleased to gather together once a year in the church and celebration. To the Atitecos the center of the church is the *r'kux ruchiliev* or umbilicus of the world the center of the world which was the birthplace of all that

The procession associated with the festival of Santiago begins and ends at the centuries old church in Santiago, Atitlan. Depicted here are members of the town's ten public cofradias, attired in their best ceremonial clothes, waiting for the procession to begin. At the foreground is the image of Santiago, the patron saint of the town. (Photo courtesy of Paul Harbaugh.)

exists. In fact there is a carefully marked hole in the center of the church that marks the spot of the center.

At a time when the mood is right the appropriate *cofradia* members bring the saints out of the church onto the front steps. In a way the celebration begins on this ancient and beautiful semicircular stairway. Around 7 AM, amidst the sounds of singing, personal greetings, and conversation, with incense floating through the morning air, *cofradia* members with their wives, family, and friends, now numbering about five hundred people, lift the platforms of saints and descend the stairs in their colorful, striking headdresses and clothes. Crowded together they slowly move across the church courtyard as *bombas* (sticks of dynamite) are lofted high into the air and explode. The percussion is so great that you must open your mouth to keep your ears from splitting in pain.

The procession is slow. It is difficult to imagine how slow the Maya move and with natural ease. They go down the stairs, slow, really slow. They proceed through the church courtyard following an imaginary line that divides the ritual space in half. This line also represents the middle of the ritual year, or ritual time. As Martin

Prechtel and I have explained in our writings, the primary symbolic function of the Atiteco *cofradia* system is to help carry the sun across the sky. Beginning at a point at the symbolic center of the year, this and other similar *cofradia* processions are understood as walking the path of the sun. To walk this path, what in Tzutujil is called "Foot of the Dawn, Foot of the Sun," is necessary for the sun's progression across the sky.

The procession, always led by a drummer and flute player, plus the litters of Santiago and two other saints, covers about 200 yards in the first half hour. Inevitably tourists are busy taking pictures and videos from different angles, while the Maya do their best to ignore them or nudge them out of the way when necessary. Once the procession leaves the churchyard it turns left, amid singing, drinking, friendly conversation, and proceeds to the first corner, where a shrine covered with pine needles houses the precious image of a saint. The procession puts all the litters down, kneels, and—following the *cabecera* or *cofradia* leader—offers prayers and the sacred beverage of *aguardiente* to the saint. This is understood as an offering that nurtures the saint, that actually feeds the little shrine and the corner of the world it represents. The *cabecera* prays hard in Tzutujil, calling out the names of deities and sacred places. Then the singers sing special prayers for roughly forty-five minutes. The group—now without the tourists, who have become bored and drifted away—has swelled in numbers of native participants. For these people believe that they are doing rituals that need to take place in this corner of the world to make the process of regeneration work.

Then, amid another series of *bomba* explosions, the procession sets off, ever so slowly, with people becoming progressively drunk to the second corner of the world. They cover about 100 yards in forty-five minutes and arrive at a second shrine. The same putting down of litters, prayers, songs, and drinking takes place for an hour or so at this shrine. Communal drinking cups are passed through the crowd, full of one of two types of alcoholic beverage. There is the *de la ley* or legal drink known as *aguardiente*. It is potent and tunes you up after a few drinks. Then there is the *contra ley* or illegal *ptzihuan ya* or "canyon water." This is very hard to drink but it cannot be refused. By now the procession consists of an intoxicated unit, a kind of Dionysian band, drunk, happy, talking serious shit loudly in each other's ears, making pledges for life, helping each other through the ritual.

At the time when the mood is right, the group, amidst the *bombas,* singing, and marimba music playing the background, sets off for the third corner of the world. But halfway to the third station, just at the point of intersection of the middle line I mentioned as we were leaving the courtyard, everyone stops and puts down the saints. This is the point of transferal of the "cargo" or religious material/responsibility from this past year's *cofradia* of Santiago to next year's group. It is immensely sad for the retiring group. Members cry, pledge lifelong faithfulness to Santiago, and speak of the power and blessing they felt during their year of having his sacred life in their care and home. *Bombas* go off as the responsibility of Santiago is transferred to his new keepers and last year's group gets up and walks away from the procession. Explicit in this ceremony is the knowledge that this transferal of care and responsibility insures the continuation of the sacred force of the saint within the human community.

Then the colorful, swaying, singing, growing throng, which by now has grown to over a thousand people, picks up the litters of saints and slowly, ever so slowly, walks to the third corner. This corner has a big house on it and the front porch serves as the shrine for the saints to be set up and worshiped. More *bombas,* drinking, prayers, feelings of commitment and unity are generated. Then it's on to the fourth corner.

Here the ritual symbolism gets complex and rich. On this corner, where the shrine would normally be, stands the Centro Americana church, the largest and oldest Protestant denomination in Guatemala. The front door of this Church stands right where the Santiago chapel should be. In fact, when the huge procession arrives, members of the church are sitting on the front steps staring smugly and disapprovingly at this "pagan" throng. So the procession goes across the street and celebrates there. And there is a *cantina* on this corner. By now the group has passed over into the rhythm of an inebriated mass, singing, swaying, praying, pledging loudly in each other's ears. Long prayers are offered, *bombas* explode, the world seems awash in color, smoke, noise, and yet a feeling of the sacred and sacrifice hovers around the group.

The ritual has gone on for over nine hours and the procession, having symbolically walked around the cosmos, returns to the area in front of the entrance to the church courtyard. Directly facing the church is the building of the municipal government and, depending on the religious and political attitudes of the mayor, the procession is either let into the courtyard of the *municipio* or made to celebrate on the steps outside. Again, prayers, toasts, the display of the saints, songs all come together with the music of a marimba band, which has been playing sacred music for hours. The group is now in the thousands. One feels surrounded, embraced, encapsulated within the atmosphere of a separate reality, intensely communal, joyful, yet on the edge of vomiting, which has taken place many times by now. It is like a time of myth when all kinds of different beings and forces came together to make the cosmos.

Then, at the right mood, the community slowly reenters the courtyard, exhausted, spent, and nearly delirious. Up until now, we have gone so slow, so slow, for ten hours going slowly. Then the devices to shoot the *bombas* into the air are collected together in an area of the courtyard. All of a sudden all the *bombas* go off in a colossal series of explosions, boom, boom, boom, boom, boom, and the entire mass rushes as fast as it can up the stairs, jostling, bumping, lifting, surging forward into the church with the litters in the lead. It is as though the rhythm of the world has been reversed from slow to rapid. This is such a powerful experience as the outside world is left behind. The saints are taken up to the main altar. More prayers, hymns, with the saints and people back at the umbilicus of the world, having traveled to and remade the cosmos. There are Indians from all over the country in the church, which is lit, in the dusk of day, with thousands of white candles.

After some time the group thins out. Members of the *cofradia* stay in the church as lines of Indians come and pray to the saints, give thanks, ask for blessings, miracles, help to end suffering, good fortune. These *cofradia* members are also guarding the saints' clothes and canopies, some of which were made in the seventeenth and eighteenth centuries of hammered silver. But they are guarding these precious items from the church officials, who they believe may try and confiscate them.

I am left with the image of Maya women, dressed with their colorful *x'kap's* or cloth halos, praying, lighting candles, singing, and eventually moving out of the ceremonial space to return home.

Amazingly, the members of the new *cofradia* of Santiago return to their ceremonial home and celebrate for three more days!

Then, five days later, the entire community repeats this walking trip around the four quarters of their universe again![16]

What can we understand, in religious terms, from this extraordinary firsthand account of the contemporary Maya pilgrimage around the cosmos? In the terms of this book at least three patterns are outstanding. First, a clear statement of cosmovision is revealed in the relationship of the people to the saints. In the Maya worldview, life is a sacred gift from the deities for which humans are responsible to nurture. As Martin Prechtel has noted, "The world is a gift, but it isn't a free gift. You must put back, if you don't do these *costumbres* (ceremonies), if you don't put things back, then the world will stop." The Maya literally believe that if they don't do these things the world will die. Something must be put back, in terms of responsible ritual actions, in order to effectively take the powers of saints and deities into one's life.

Second, this ritual helps us understand one of the major patterns in Mesoamerican religions, namely sacrifice. For the Maya to carry out this ritual, extraordinary sacrifices are made. The Maya say this ritual involves *sacrificio* in terms of the serious expense incurred by the *cofradia* members who care for, nurture, and pay some of the expenses of this and other rituals. Also, the drinking to full drunkenness is difficult, painful, and has a stunning effect for weeks afterward. This drunkenness is a *passage* into the sacred time of Santiago, a time marked by the theme of division of realities. Just as Santiago has the capacity to divide things in two so that they become more abundant, the ritual drunkenness makes one's sense of self, community, time, and health more abundant, multivalent, larger. This is also a sacrifice because of the pain, vomiting, in fact "ritual illness," which is incurred in order to take someone to another level of reality. In this ritual the Maya, as Carlsen makes so clear, exhaust their financial and emotional resources in order to become reduced to a basic economic, social, and emotional community, which is in the process of starting over, fresh and full of new potency.

Third, the action of responsible ritual care and sacrifice is done in order to renew the cosmos. This worldrenewing is done by symbolically retracing the cosmic image of the center and the four quarters. It is significant that the cosmology of great cities such as Teotihuacan, Tollan, and Tenochtitlan, with their ceremonial centers and four cardinal directions, is replicated in the microcosm of the block surrounding the main church in Santiago Atitlan.

Conclusions

We have, like the pilgrims in Santiago Atitlan, come full circle. In our introductory chapter we noticed that the study of Mesoamerican religions is the study of ceremonial centers where peoples acted out the dramas of their cosmovisions, which outlined the relations of celestial and human beings. In each historical period, Olmec, Maya, Teotihuacan, Toltec, and Aztec peoples built monumental ceremonial cities inscribed with images and symbols of their intimate relations with supernatural forces. We have seen how the human body, mountains, stars, kings, warriors, ancestors, language, buildings, plants, and the underworld were experienced and viewed as living containers of spiritual power originating above and below the human level of existence. And we have witnessed the various ritual means used by humans to make, center, and renew their cosmos in a multiplicity of ceremonial centers. In the post-conquest setting, characterized by surprising continuities and ingenious changes, we have seen how new combinations of native and European religious elements were joined to create new types of ceremonial centers in homes, in deserts, at pre-Columbian sites and surrounding Christian churches. Like the Atiteco Maya we have circumambulated a part of the history of religions in Mesoamerica. At every stop we find a ceremonial center orienting religious experience and expression.

It is important to remember that one of the most distinctive aspects of the history of Mesoamerican religions is its relationship to the urban world and primary urban generation. The religious patterns that helped give birth to the Mesoamerican urban tradition are one of the keys to understanding the role of religion in what scholars have called the "birth of civilization" in human experience. In studying the religions of Mesoamerica we are observing and interpreting one of the greatest transformations and developments in the imagination and social organization of the human species. In social terms we are studying the role of religion in the emergence and development of hierarchical societies organized on a political and territorial basis around monumental ceremonial centers that served as the quintessential sacred meeting points between supernatural forces and human life. In a way, by studying Mesoamerican religions as we have in this book, we are studying the formation and history of that great artifact, the city, which, though it has undergone many significant transformations, is the setting we live in today.

But what is the future of Mesoamerica and its religious imagination? The pattern of the future can be seen in the patterns of its past. Both Mesoamerican cosmology and history were characterized by "eccentric periodicities," meaning periods of stability forcefully interrupted by collapses, rebellions, violent transformations, and new beginnings. Some people consider the reign of the Virgin of Guadalupe as the Sixth Age or Sun of central Mesoamerica. And with the prodigious complexities of change taking place in parts of Latin America today, we will likely see more rather than fewer manifestations of syncretism appearing in new reports, anthropological research, and creative literature. Mesoamerican religions today constitute one of the great fields for the study of social and religious change, innovation, and persistence. As the cults of Guadalupe, Santiago, and the peyote hunt demonstrate, even when a new urban tradition (European) was imposed on Mesoamerica, ancient ritual patterns competed with the more powerful (politically speaking) theological ideas for a significant place in the novel combinations that emerged. With new technologies and weapons spreading across Mesoamerica it is very difficult to know what the future holds, what kind of city, what forms the cults of Guadalupe, Santiago, and the peyote hunt will take. It follows from the approach of this book that as long as they have their ceremonial centers for worship, orientation, and vision they will continue to mix native and imposed religious patterns.

There is also an ironic dimension to the conquest of the indigenous urban tradition by the Europeans. Every year in Mesoamerican cities and in rural areas were ancient cities once stood, new discoveries of ruins awaken the modern sensibility to the haunting presence of the pre-Columbian ceremonial world. When the subway was installed in Mexico City in the 1960s through 1980s impressive finds of temples, burials, and statues continually made the news. In a sense the more modern Mesoamerica becomes, the more it will recover its pre-Hispanic roots. As Carlos Fuentes stated about modern Mexico City, it is a "city ancient in light . . . city witness to all we forget."

One of the most interesting responses to the changes of the modern West comes from the Chicano movement in the United States. This response includes the utilization and celebration of the pre-Hispanic past in the aesthetic and political expressions for Chicano liberation in the United States. Chicanos are Americans of Mexican descent who have formed a movement to liberate themselves from Anglo stereotypes, political oppression, poverty, unqual opportunity, and spiritual doubt. This movement, also called the Chicano Renaissance, was most vocally represented in the Farmworkers' Union led by Cesar Chavez, in the Centro de la Raza led by Corky Gonzalez in Denver, and by the movement to recover ancestral lands in New Mexico. It receives its most vivid expression in the music, mural art work, and community services programs found in every Chicano community from El Paso, Texas, to Washington, D.C. Over the course of this movement there has been a remarkable interest and representation of Aztec, Maya, Olmec, and Teotihuacan symbolism. In Chicago's Pilsen Community, for instance, where Chicanos have gained important political power, stands Casa Aztlan, an all-purpose community center housing colorful murals depicting Mexican history from the time of the Toltecs to the present. Casa Aztlan (the Home of Aztlan) is named after the mythical homeland, north of the Aztec capital, from which the Mexica ancestors left in order to build their great center, Tenochtitlan. Chicanos in Chicago claim that that original homeland is their *barrio,* where struggle and celebration are joined in a movement to ease the pain of urban living. They know in their minds that, geographically speaking, Aztlan is much further south. But in the religious imagination a sacred place can be anywhere there is a revelation of the spiritual resources and destiny of a people. Casa Aztlan is a modern-day ceremonial center for Chicanos to recall the pre-Columbian past and use that recall to strengthen themselves. In every Chicano community in the United States there are educational projects (some named after Quetzalcoatl), political movements (some named after Cuauhtemoc), and cultural centers (named after the Toltecs or the Mayas) that reflect a reaching back for power and inspiration from distant ancestors who, like the family spirits in the Dia de los Muertos, are given a path to reenter the world of the living. It is a special gift of the religious imagination that allows a people, after five hundred years of colonialism, dependency, oppression, and resistance, to turn to the ancient Mesoamerican past for symbols of a cosmovision that help make a world meaningful, give it a standing center, and provide for social and spiritual renewal.

And this Chicano example of utilizing the creative past for regeneration in the present is part of a wider significance to be found in studying Mesoamerica. To study its ceremonial cities and religious imagination leads us to consider comparisons with other ancient urban traditions. And to consider Mesoamerica's unique colonial history leads us to realize just how novel the New World was and is. As Díaz del Castillo wrote long ago, when reminiscing about his youthful attacks on the Aztec capital,

> And some of our soldiers even asked whether the things that we saw were not a dream. It is not to be wondered at that I here write it down in this manner, for there is so much to think over that I do not know how to describe it, seeing things as we did that had never been heard of or seen before, not even dreamed about.

Of course the native Mesoamericans had never dreamed of the European world, either, and when the two came together they created a wonderfully complex world that we must continue to strive to understand and appreciate. It is the purpose of this small book to help us understand and appreciate Mesoamerican religions, not only because they are Mesoamerican but also because they reveal to us dimensions of the human imagination and its expression in the work of the human body.

Notes

Preface

1. Tzvetan Todorov, *The Conquest of America: The Question of the Other* (New York: Harper & Row, 1982), 4.

2. Bernal Díaz del Castillo, *The Discovery and Conquest of Mexico* (New York: Farrar, Straus & Giroux, 1956), 191.

3. Miguel Leon-Portilla, *The Broken Spears* (Boston: Beacon Press, 1962), 138.

4. Paul Wheatley, *The Pivot of the Four Quarters: A Preliminary Enquiry into the Origins and Nature of the Ancient Chinese City* (Chicago: Aldine, 1971), especially chapter 3.

5. The "blood of kings" is the title of an outstanding book on Maya religion, *The Blood of Kings: Dynasty and Ritual in Maya Art* by Linda Schele and Mary Ellen Miller. (Fort Worth: Kimbell Art Museum, 1986).

I. Introduction: Approaching Mesoamerican Religions

1. Inga Clendinnen, *Ambivalent Conquests: Maya and Spaniard in Yucatan, 1517–1570* (Cambridge: Cambridge University Press, 1988), iii.

2. J. H. Elliott, *The Old World and the New: 1492–1650* (Cambridge: Cambridge Unviersity Press, 1970), 1.

3. *First Images of America: The Impact of the New World on the Old.* (Berkeley: University of California Press, 1976), vol.1, 14.

4. Miguel Leon-Portilla, *The Broken Spears* (Boston: Beacon Press, 1962), 51–52.

5. Lewis B. Hanke, *Aristotle and the American Indians: A Study in Race Prejudice in the Modern World* (Bloomington: University of Indiana Press, 1959), 38.

6. Diego Durán, *Book of the Gods and the Rites and the Ancient Calendar,* trans. and ed. Doris Heyden and Fernando Horcasitas (Norman: University of Oklahoma Press, 1970), 51.

7. Hanke, *Aristotle,* 47.

8. Quoted in Davíd Carrasco, "City as Symbol in Aztec Religion: Clues from the *Codex Mendoza,*" *History of Religions Journal, 20,* No. 3 (February/1981): 200.

9. Miguel Leon-Portilla, *Native Mesoamerican Spirituality* (New York: Paulist Press, 1980), 201.

10. Durán, *Book of the Gods,* 70.

11. Bernardino de Sahagun, *The Florentine Codex: General History of the Things of New Spain,* ed. Arthur J. O. Anderson and Charles Dibble, 12 vols. (Sante Fe, NM: School of American Research and University of Utah, 1950–1969), vol. II, 103.

12. Bernal Díaz del Castillo, *The Discovery and Conquest of Mexico* (New York: Farrar, Straus & Giroux, 1956), 222.

II. History and Cosmovision in Mesoamerican Religions

1. Munro S. Edmonson, *The Book of Counsel: The Popol Vuh of the Quiche Maya of Guatemala* (New Orleans: Middle American Research Institute, Tulane University, 1971), 148.

2. Henry T. Wright, "Mesopotamia to Mesoamerica," *Archaeology* (January/February 1989).

3. Bernardino de Sahagun, *The Florentine Codex: General History of the Things of New Spain,* ed. Arthur J. O. Anderson and Charles Dibble, 12 vols. (Sante Fe, NM: School of American Research and University of Utah), 127.

4. Kent V. Flannery, "Contextual Analysis of Ritual Paraphernalia from Formative Oaxaca," in *The Early Mesoamerican Village,* ed. Kent V. Flannery (New York: Academic Press), 333–45.

5. Diego Durán, *Book of the Gods and the Rites and the Ancient Calendar,* trans. and ed. Doris Heyden and Fernando Horcasitas (Norman: University of Oklahoma Press, 1970), 314.

6. Linda Schele and Mary Ellen Miller, *The Blood of Kings: Dynasty and Ritual in Maya Art* (Fort Worth: Kimbell Art Museum, 1986), 318.

7. Sahagun, *Florentine Codex,* Book VII, 4.

8. *Ibid.,* Book III, 39.

9. *Ibid.,* Book X, 166.

10. *Ibid.,* 168.

11. Miguel Leon-Portilla, *Precolumbian Literatures of Mexico* (Norman: University of Oklahoma Press, 1969), 87.

12. Alfredo Lopez Austin, *The Human Body and Ideology: Concepts Among the Ancient Nahuas,* trans. Bernardo Ortiz de Montellano (Salt Lake City: University of Utah Press, 1988), 57.

13. *Ibid.,* 65.

III. The Religion of the Aztecs: Ways of the Warrior, Words of the Priest

1. Bernardino de Sahagun, *The Florentine Codex: General History of the Things of New Spain,* ed. Arthur J. O. Anderson and Charles Dibble, 12 vols. (Santa Fe, NM: School of American Research and University of Utah, 1950–1969), Book III, 15.

2. See Davíd Carrasco, *Quetzalcoatl and the Irony of Empire: Myths and Prophecies in the Aztec Tradition* (Chicago, University of Chicago Press, 1982). The authoritative work on the Toltec tradition is H. B. Nicholson, "Topiltzin Quetzalcoatl of Tollan: A Problem in Mesoamerican Ethnohistory", Ph.D. diss., Harvard University, 1957.

3. Diego Durán, *The Book of the Gods and the Rites and The Ancient Calendar,* trans. and ed. Doris Heyden and Fernando Horcasitas (Norman: University of Oklahoma Press, 1970), 59.

4. *Anales de Cuauhtitlan,* quoted in Miguel Leon-Portilla, *Native Mesoamerican Spirituality* (New York: Paulist Press, 1980), 169.

5. *Leyenda de los Soles,* trans. John Bierhorst, *Four Masterworks of American Indian Literature* (New York: Farrar, Straus & Giroux, 1974), 21.

6. *Anales de Cuauhtitlan,* in *Ibid.,* 29.

7. *Ibid.*

8. Sahagun, *Florentine Codex,* Book X, 166.

9. *Ibid.*

10. *Anales de Cuauhtitlan,* quoted in Bierhorst, *Four Masterpieces,* 62.

11. Sahagun, *Florentine Codex,* Book VI, 25.

12. Alfredo Lopez Austin, *The Human Body and Ideology: Concepts Among the Ancient Nahuas,* trans. Bernardo Ortiz de Montellano (Salt Lake City: University of Utah Press, 1988), 328.

13. Bernal Díaz del Castillo, *The Discovery and Conquest of Mexico* (New York: Farrar, Straus & Giroux, 1956), 436. See also the many works by Johanna Broda on sacred mountains.

14. All the quotes in this section about the birth of Huitzilopochtli come from Book III of Sahagun's *Florentine Codex.* I am using Leon-Portilla's more literary translation as found in *Native Mesoamerican Spirituality,* 220–25.

15. Sahagun, *Florentine Codex: Introduction and Indices,* 65.

16. Leon-Portilla, *Mesoamerican Spirituality,* 241–42.

17. *Ibid.,* 243.

18. *Ibid.*

19. Sahagun, *Florentine Codex,* Book VI, 167.

20. *Ibid.,* 113–18.

21. Leon-Portilla, *Mesoamerican Spirituality,* 63–64.

22. All the riddles in this section are from Book VI of Sahagun, *Florentine Codex,* 237–40.

23. *Ibid.,* 219–35.

24. *Ibid.,* Book VII, 26.

25. *Ibid.,* Book II, 67.

26. *Ibid.,* 71.

27. *Ibid.,* 71.

IV. Maya Religion: Cosmic Trees, Sacred Kings, and the Underworld

1. Dennis Tedlock, *Popul Vuh* (New York: Simon & Schuster, 1985), 163.

2. Linda Schele and Mary Ellen Miller, *The Blood of Kings: Dynasty and Ritual in Maya Art* (Fort Worth: Kimbell Art Museum, 1986), 300.

3. John L. Stephens, *Incidents of Travel in Central America, Chiapas and Yucatan* (London: 1844), 82–83.

4. Dennis Tedlock, *Popul Vuh* (New York: Simon & Schuster, 1985), 73.

5. *Ibid.,* 181.

6. Mircea Eliade, *Patterns in Comparative Religions* (New York: Meridian Books, 1963), 345.

7. Robert S. Carlsen and Martin Prechtel, "The Flowering of the Dead: Mayan Notions of Sacred Change," unpublished manuscript, 5.

8. In this section I have utilized the remarkable achievements in interpreting the Maya by Schele and Miller in *The Blood of Kings*.

9. Tedlock, *Popul Vuh,* 71.

10. *Ibid.,* 72.

11. *Ibid.*

12. *Ibid.,* 79.

13. Schele and Miller, *The Blood of Kings,* 181.

14. Michael Coe, *The Maya* (New York: Praeger, 1973), 58.

15. See a series of works by Anthony F. Aveni, especially *Skywatchers of Ancient Mexico* (Austin: University of Texas Press, 1980).

16. Tedlock, *Popul Vuh,* 134.

17. *Ibid.,* 147.

18. *Ibid.,* 152.

19. *Ibid.,* 160.

20. Miguel Leon-Portilla, *Native Mesoamerican Spirituality* (New York: Paulist Press, 1980), 134.

V. Mesoamerica as a New World: Colonialism and Religious Creativity

1. William B. Taylor, "Between Global Process and Local Knowl-

edge: An Inquiry into Early Latin American Social History, 1500–1900" in *Reliving the Past: The Worlds of Social History,* ed. Oliver Zunz (Chapel Hill: University of North Carolina Press, 1985), 116.

2. Carlos Fuentes, *Where the Air Is Clear* (New York: Farrar, Straus & Giroux, 1971), 5.

3. Elizabeth Wilder Weismann, *Mexico in Sculpture 1521–1821* (Cambridge, Harvard University Press, 1950), 5.

4. For a general discussion of religious syncretism see the article on Syncretism in the *Encyclopedia of Religion,* general ed. Mircea Eliade (New York: Macmillan, 1987), 218–26.

5. Quoted in Tzvetan Todorov, *The Conquest of America: The Question of Other* (New York: Harper & Row, 1982), 138.

6. *Ibid.,* 141.

7. Taylor, "Global Process," 117.

8. *Ibid.,* 123.

9. Carol Karasik, ed., Robert M. Laughlin, collector and trans., *The People of the Bat: Mayan Tales and Dreams from Zincantan* (Washington, D.C.: Smithsonian Institution Press, 1988), 137–38.

10. William B. Taylor, "The Virgin of Guadalupe in New Spain: An Inquiry into the Social History of Marian Devotion," *American Ethnologist,* 9–33.

11. Barbara Meyerhoff, *Peyote Hunt: The Sacred Journey of the Huichol Indians* (Ithaca: Cornell University Press, 1974), 33.

12. *Ibid.,* 147.

13. *Ibid.,* 153.

14. Quoted in Hugo Nutini, *Todos Santos in Rural Tlaxcala: A Syncretic, Expressive, and Symbolic Analysis of the Cult of the Dead* (Princeton: Princeton University Press, 1988), 56.

15. *Ibid.,* 152.

16. Robert Carlsen, a Ph.D. student at the University of Colorado, personal interview.

Glossary

altepetl. Mountain filled with water. The Aztec term meaning a community or city.

autosacrifice. The bleeding of one's own body (tongue, earlobes, thighs, genitals, and so on) as an offering to the gods, or as a means to induce a vision of a supernatural being or ancestor. Autosacrifice was often associated with legitimation of royalty.

Bonampak. Classic Maya ceremonial center discovered in 1946. It contained a number of monumental buildings, including one palace whose interior walls were covered with murals depicting courtly life, warfare, ceremonial processions, and ritual sacrifice associated with continuity of the royal lineage.

calendar round. A fifty-two year period determined by the intermeshing of the 260-day ritual calendar and the 365-day solar calendar. All possible combinations of the two calendars are exhausted after 18,980 days, equaling fifty-two years.

cemanahuac. "Land surrounded by water." The Aztec term for the terrestrial level of the cosmos.

ceremonial center. The ritual and spatial center of Mesoamerican homes, cities, and communities, where the cosmovision was expressed in decoration, sculpture, painting, and ritual performance. In urban societies the major ceremonial centers consisted of monumental buildings including pyramids, temples, stairways, stelae, ball courts, palaces.

Chac-Xib-Chac. The Maya god of war, sacrifice, and dancing.

Chichimecas. From *chichi,* "dog"; and *mecatl,* "rope" or "lineage." A general term for the migrating tribes who settled in the valley of Mexico (including Tenochtitlan and Tlatelolco) in the twelfth and thirteenth centuries.

Classic Maya. The Maya culture of 200–900 CE, which

achieved extraordinarily complex mathematical, calendrical, astronomical, architectural traditions organized in ceremonial cities in southern Mexico, Guatemala, Honduras, and other locations.

Coatepec. Serpent Mountain. The mythical mountain where Coatlicue, Lady of the Serpent Skirt, gave birth to the Aztec patron god, Huitzilopochtli, Hummingbird on the Left. The Aztecs gave this name to their greatest shrine, the Templo Mayor of Tenochtitlan.

cosmovision. A worldview that integrates the structure of space and the rhythms of time into a unified whole. See photographs of the Sun Stone and the Codex Ferjérváry Mayer for examples.

Coyolxauhqui. The female warrior who led the attack against Coatlicue in the Aztec mythic episode of Huitzilopochtli's birth.

Cuauhtemoc. Diving Eagle. The last Aztec ruler who resisted the Spanish attack on Tlatelolco. A nephew of Motecuhzoma Xocoyotzin.

Dia de los Muertos. Day of the Dead. Yearly celebrations during the end of October and beginning of November that celebrate the reunion of the souls of the dead with living family members and friends.

ecological complex. The context of urban centers consisting of the human population, agriculture, geography, technology, and social stratification.

Florentine Codex. The twelve-volume encyclopedia of Aztec life describing the supernatural, human, and natural world of pre-Columbian central Mesoamerica. Compiled by Bernardino de Sahagun with the help of native informants.

hombre-dios. Man-god. A Spanish term referring to the native idea of human beings imbued with special capacities to communicate with and contain the will of deities within their hearts.

huehuetlatolli. The Ancient Word or Sayings of the Elders. Elegant, florid, rhetorical orations representing the traditional teachings about ethics, aesthetics, symbolism, politics, and authority in the Aztec world.

Hunahpu and Xbalanque. The Hero Twins of the *Popul Vuh*. They successfully undergo the ordeals of Xibalba, the Maya underworld.

in xochitl, in cuicatl.   Flower and song. An Aztec term meaning poetry, the Truth on earth.

Lady Xoc.   Maya royal person (ritual partner of Yaxchilán's Shield Jaguar), who is depicted in sculpture carrying out autosacrifice and having a vision of an ancestral warrior.

las Casas, Bartolome de.   The Bishop of Chiapas, who defended the natives of Mesoamerica in the debates of Valladolid, Spain, in 1550–1555.

La Venta.   An early (1500–800 BCE) Olmec ceremonial center containing one of the earliest pyramids in Mesoamerica.

Long Count.   The Maya calendar system, which utilized the concept of zero to calculate the passage of time by marking five units of measurement, constructed in part to relate contemporary rulers to an ancient chain of ancestors.

Mah K'ina.   Great Sun Lords, the title of Maya rulers in the Classic period.

mara'akame.   Huichol shaman who guides the pilgrims on the peyote hunt, knows the sacred traditions of the community and heals.

Maya collapse.   Classic Maya civilization disintegrated rapidly between 790-900 CE. Its causes are still only partially understood.

Mictlan.   Region of the Dead. The ninth level of the Aztec underworld, where the souls of people who died ordinary deaths resided.

millennial kingdom.   The Franciscan idea (derived from the Book of Revelation) that the thorough conversion of the Indians would result in the realization of heaven on earth.

Moctezuma.   The modern name given to the two Aztec rulers, Moteuczoma Ilhuicamina (1440–1454) and Moteuczoma Xocoyotzin (1503–1519)

Mountain of Sustenance.   A mythic mountain that was the source of abundance, rain, seeds, corn, food. This mountain was symbolized in the Tlaloc section of the Great Temple of Tenochtitlan.

Myth of the Suns.   The story of the four ages of the cosmos leading up to the Fifth Age of the Aztecs.

New Fire Ceremony.   The ceremony held once every fifty-two years to mark the passage of one major cycle into another. All fires were extinguished and a new fire representing a new time period was lit at the precise astronomical moment.

nextlaoaliztli.   The Aztec term for debt-payment, which often took the form of elaborate ceremonies lasting twenty days and culminating in human sacrifices.

Nezahualcoyotl.   Fasting Coyote. The Aztec Tlatoani or Chief Speaker of the cultural capital of Texcoco.

nim q'ij Santiag.   Big Sun Santiago was the Atiteco Maya name for the feast of Santiago, in which the participants circumambulate the town block around the cathedral to renew the cosmos.

Olmec Style.   The extraordinary artistic and political style of Olmec culture (1500 BCE–300 BCE) characterized by the reshaping of earth materials into a religious cosmovision. The Olmec emphasized jade and stone work depicting animal and animal/human combinations. The Olmec influence spread throughout many parts of Mesoamerica during the Formative Period.

Ometeotl.   Aztec God of Duality, who resided in the highest level of heaven from which he/she created the cosmos and continually creates life.

Pacal.   Seventh-century Maya ruler of Palenque, whose tomb depicts the descent of the ruler into the underworld.

Palenque.   Beautiful Maya ceremonial center (fourth–ninth centuries CE). It contains a series of temples known as the Group of the Cross, which depict the Maya cosmology in detail. The site of Pacal's tomb.

Pleiades.   Star cluster, which the Aztecs called Tianquitzli (Marketplace). Its movements had influence on the spatial layout of cities and the ritual calendars of Mesoamerica.

Popul Vuh.   *Book of Council* of the Quiché Maya, discovered in Chichicastenango, Guatemala, in 1701. It contains a rich account of cosmovision and ritual actions of preconquest and postconquest Maya peoples.

primary urban generation.   The complex process of original urban formation in Mesoamerica, China, Egypt, Mesopotamia, Indus Valley, Nigeria, Peru.

Quetzalcoatl. The Plumed Serpent or Precious Twin was a Toltec and Aztec god. One of the four sons of Ometeotl, who created the cosmos and ruled over periods of its history.

r'kux ruchiliev. Umbilicus of the world located in the center of the Atiteco Maya cosmos.

Sahagun, Bernardino de. The Franciscan priest whose research and writing (in Nahuatl and Spanish) on Nahuatl/Aztec culture resulted in the *Florentine Codex: The General History of Things in New Spain.*

Sepulveda, Juan Ginés de. Spanish philosopher, who utilized Aristotle's vision of social relations to argue that the natives of Mesoamerica were slaves by nature.

special assemblages. Groups of buildings misaligned in relation to other buildings but aligned to enable viewers to see important astronomical events along the horizon.

syncretism. The complex process by which rituals, beliefs, and symbols from different religions are combined to create new meanings. Syncretism is most clearly represented in ritual performances that enable people to locate themselves within the new world of meaning.

Templo Mayor. Great Temple. A number of Aztec communities had a Templo Mayor, but this term usually refers to the Great Aztec Temple of Tenochtitlan.

Tenochtitlan. Place of the Prickly Pear Cactus, the capital city of the Aztec empire, founded around 1325 and conquered by the Spanish in 1521. Site of Mexico City.

Teotihuacan. Place Where the Gods Were Born. The imperial capital of second to seventh century CE central Mesoamerica. Known today as the pyramids, it was populated by over 200,000 people. The Aztec considered it the place where the Fifth Sun was created.

teotl ixiptla. Aztec term meaning image of a god. These images were sometimes humans, usually destined for sacrifice in one of the major festivals of the Aztec calendar.

teyolia. Aztec term for a spiritual force that resided in the human heart and provided the person with intelligence, fondness, inclinations.

tlachco. The Aztec ball court where the sacred ball game was played.

Tlaloc. The rain god who brought moisture, fertility, and regeneration, and whose powers resided in mountains, caves, and the fertile earth. Tlaloc's major shrine was at the Templo Mayor of Tenochtitlan.

tlamatinime. Knowers of Things. These Aztec wisemen used language arts to seek and teach profound truths.

Tlatelolco. The sister city of Tenochtitlan. It became the site of the imperial marketplace and a major ceremonial center.

Tollan. Place of Reeds. This was the fabulous Toltec City (ninth-eleventh centuries CE).

tonalli. Spiritual force sent by the Aztec god Ometeotl, the sun, and fire into the human body, giving it character, intelligence, and will. *Tonalli* was concentrated in the head of humans.

Topiltzin Quetzalcoatl. Our Young Prince the Feathered Serpent. The priest ruler of Tollan, whose career became a model for Aztec rulers, priests, and artists.

Toxcatl. Dry Season. The Aztec festival dedicated to Tezcatlipoca, Lord of the Smoking Mirror, in which the teotl ixiptla, image of the god, paraded through the capital for one year prior to his sacrifice.

Tzutujil. The Maya community residing in and around Santiago Atitlan in Guatemala.

Virgin of Guadalupe. The patron saint of Mexico appeared to the Indian Juan Diego near the Aztec shrine of Tepeyac in 1531. She is the loving guardian, intermediary to God, and courageous warrior of the faithful.

Wirikuta. The ancestral land of peyote for the Huichol peoples of Mexico. Each year pilgrimages under the guidance of *mara'akame* go to Wirikuta to renew, through peyote visions, their community.

Xibalba. The Maya underworld was a place of ordeals and transformations where the Hero Twins overcame the Lords of the Dead. The place through which all people must travel in order to be regenerated.

Xiuhtecuhtli. The Aztec Fire God who dwelled at the center of homes, ceremonial centers, communities, and the cosmos.

Xochiyaoyotl. Wars of the Flowers were a series of scheduled battlefield confrontations between the Aztecs and enemy city-states. Their purpose was to reestablish political balance, train warriors, and supply sacrificial victims.

zempoalxochitl. Marigolds cultivated for Day of the Dead celebrations in Mexico. They decorate altars and are laid out to mark a path, which the dead souls can smell and thus follow during their return to the human community.

Selected Reading List

Adams, Robert McC. *The Evolution of Urban Society.* Chicago: Aldine Press, 1967.

Aveni, Anthony F. *Skywatchers of Ancient Mexico.* Austin: University of Texas Press, 1980.

Bernal, Ignacio. *The Olmec World.* Berkeley: University of California Press, 1969.

Boone, Elizabeth Hill. *The Codex Magliabechiano.* 2 vols. Berkeley: University of California Press, 1983.

Broda, Johanna, Davíd Carrasco, and Eduardo Matos Moctezuma. *The Great Temple of Tenochtitlan.* Berkeley: University of California Press, 1987.

Brundage, Burr. *The Fifth Sun.* Austin: University of Texas Press, 1979.

Calnek, Edward. "The Internal Structure of Tenochtitlan" in *The Valley of Mexico,* ed. Eric Wolf. Albuquerque: University of New Mexico Press, 1976.

Carrasco, Davíd. *Quetzalcoatl and the Irony of Empire. Myths and Prophecies in the Aztec Tradition.* Chicago: University of Chicago Press, 1982.

Coe, Michael. *The Maya.* 3d. ed. New York: Thames and Hudson, 1984.

Culbert, T. Patrick, ed. *The Classic Maya Collapse.* Albuquerque: University of New Mexico Press, 1973.

Díaz del Castillo, Bernal. *The Discovery and Conquest of Mexico.* New York: Farrar, Straus & Giroux, 1956.

Durán, Diego. *Book of the Gods and the Rites and the Ancient Calendar.* Trans. and ed. by Fernando Horcasitas and Doris Heyden. Norman: University of Oklahoma Press, 1970.

Edmonson, Munro S. *The Ancient Future of the Itza.* Austin: University of Texas Press, 1982.

Elliott, J. H. *The Old World and the New: 1492–1650.* Cambridge: Cambridge University Press, 1970.

Gossen, Gary H. *Chamulas in the World of the Sun.* Cambridge, Harvard University Press, 1974.

Hanke, Lewis. *Aristotle and the American Indians. A Study in Race Prejudice in the Modern World.* Bloomington: Indiana University Press, 1959.

Heyden, Doris. "An Interpretation of the Cave Underneath the Pyramid of the Sun in Teotihuacan, Mexico." *American Antiquity* 40(2) (1975): 131–47.

Katz, Friedrich. *Ancient American Civilizations.* New York: Praeger, 1972.

Keen, Benjamin. *The Aztec Image in Western Thought.* New Brunswick, NJ: Rutgers University Press, 1971.

Klein, Cecelia. "Who was Tlaloc?" *Journal of Latin American Lore* 6(2) (1980): 155-204.

Landa, Diego de. *Relacion de las Cosas de Yucatan.* Ed. Alfred Tozzer. Cambridge: Harvard University Press, 1941.

Leon-Portilla, Miguel. *Aztec Thought and Culture.* Norman: University of Oklahoma Press, 1963.

———. *Native Mesoamerican Spirituality.* New York: Paulist Press, 1980.

Lopez Austin, Alfredo. *Hombre-Dios: Religion y Politica en el Mundo Nahuatl.* Mexico: Universidad Nacional Autonoma de Mexico, 1973.

———. *Human Body and Ideology.* Trans. Bernardo Ortiz de Montellano. Salt Lake City: University of Utah Press, 1988.

Matos Moctezuma, Eduardo. *El Templo Mayor: Excavaciones y Estudios.* Mexico: Instituto Nacional de Antropología y Historia, 1982.

Millon, Rene. *Urbanization at Teotihuacan, Mexico: The Teotihuacan Map.* Austin: University of Texas Press, 1973.

Nicholson, H. B. "Religion in Pre-Hispanic Central Mexico." In

Handbook of Middle American Indians 10: 395–445. Austin: University of Texas Press, 1964–1976.

Pasztory, Esther. *Aztec Art*. New York: Henry N. Abrams, 1983.

Paz, Octavio. *The Other Mexico*. New York: Grove Press, 1972.

Sahagun, Fray Bernardino de. *The Florentine Codex: General History of the Things of New Spain*. Ed. Arthur J. O. Anderson and Charles Dibble. 12 vols. Sante Fe, NM: School of American Research and University of Utah, 1950–1969.

Schele, Linda and Mary Ellen Miller. *The Blood of Kings: Dynasty and Ritual in Maya Art*. Fort Worth: Kimbell Art Museum, 1986.

Stuart, George E. and Gene S. Stuart. *The Mysterious Maya*. Washington, D. C.: National Geographic Society, 1977.

Tedlock, Dennis. *Popul Vuh*. New York: Simon & Schuster, 1985.

Townsend, Richard. *State and Cosmos in the Art of Tenochtitlan*. Studies in Pre-Columbian Art and Archaeology 20. Washington, D. C.: Dumbarton Oaks, Trustees for Harvard University, 1979.

van der Loo, Peter. *Codices, Costumbres, Continuidad*. Leiden, 1987.

Weismann, Elizabeth Wilder. *Mexico in Sculpture: 1521–1821*. Cambridge: Harvard University Press, 1950.

Wheatley, Paul. *The Pivot of the Four Quarters: A Preliminary Enquiry into the Origins and Nature of the Ancient Chinese City*. Chicago: Aldine, 1971.